THE WET WOUND

AN ELEGY IN ESSAYS

MADDIE NORRIS

THE UNIVERSITY OF
GEORGIA PRESS
ATHENS

Author's note: Some names have been changed to protect identities.

Published by the University of Georgia Press
Athens, Georgia 30602
www.ugapress.org
© 2024 by Maddie Norris
All rights reserved
Designed by Kaelin Chappell Broaddus
Set in 10.25/13.5 Miller Text Roman by Kaelin Chappell Broaddus
Printed digitally
Most University of Georgia Press titles are
available from popular e-book vendors.

Printed in the United States of America
24 25 26 27 28 P 5 4 3 2 1

Library of Congress Cataloging-in-Publication Data

Names: Norris, Maddie, 1994– author.
Title: The wet wound : an elegy in essays / Maddie Norris.
Description: Athens, Georgia : University of Georgia Press, [2024]
| Series: Crux: the Georgia series in literary nonfiction
Identifiers: LCCN 2023037536 | ISBN 9780820366685 (paperback ; alk.
paper) | ISBN 9780820366692 (epub) | ISBN 9780820366708 (pdf)
Subjects: LCSH: Norris, Maddie, 1994– | Grief. | Loss
(Psychology) | Parents—Death—Psychological aspects.
Classification: LCC BF575.G7 .N675 2024 | DDC 155.9/37—dc23/eng/20230928
LC record available at https://lccn.loc.gov/2023037536

For Dad, as always

Loquela
This word, borrowed from Ignatius of Loyola,
designates the flux of language through which the
subject tirelessly rehashes the effects of a wound
—ROLAND BARTHES

CONTENTS

THE WET WOUND

HYPERBARIC, OR HOW TO KEEP A WOUND ALIVE

n 1960, twenty-seven piglets didn't die. Their blood was removed, each platelet sucked out and replaced with Ringer's fluid, a solution of salts dissolved in water. The soft pink skins of pigs rested in a hyperbaric oxygen chamber with three times the air pressure at sea-level closing in on them. Their bodies were bundled in air. For the better part of an hour, they breathed pure oxygen. After forty-five minutes, the animals were removed, and blood relayed back to them. Twenty-seven piglets lived without blood for forty-five minutes. There were no long-lasting symptoms to show they'd lived life without what was considered vital, no lingering side effects from living without what keeps us alive. The piglets went on to live full lives. In 1960, the year my dad was born, twenty-seven piglets didn't die.

After Dad died, Mom drove to the hospital to pack up his office, then returned home to store the stuffed boxes in her old study. When my grandmother died, my dad's mom, we got more of his things, more ligaments of a life thrown into a box, carried in a car, and placed in a room. Cups, letters, Mother's Day cards signed "Love, Tom." Medical reference books, framed family photos, grades from elementary school. A *Big Lebowski* rug mousepad, floppy discs embedded with patient information, a poem I wrote for him.

Physically, it was hard to enter Mom's former study; the boxes spread up and across, asphyxiating the room. They stacked up and settled into each other, like a tower of blocks a child might have built: solid and precarious. Light swept through the windows and scanned the brown cardboard day in and day out. Nothing else touched them. No one looked through them. They stayed closed for roughly half a decade.

Then, one December, in the cold weeks before Christmas, it rained for days on end, and the roof couldn't take it. Its body punched open, and water leaked in. The wood around the windows swelled with liquid, and the paint flaked open like a hundred razored cuts. We needed to clear the study so the wall could be repaired.

My brother and I were on break from college, and we waded into the room behind Mom. It had been seven years. Will's hair was close-cropped, and he moved with military efficiency, picking up boxes, carrying them into the hall, and putting them down, while I tried to make myself as small as possible, crouching to examine a paperweight, a notebook, a pen. Mom was somewhere between, drawn by the memories but wary of the way they pulled her under. She kept moving. In one long day, the three of us went through the boxes full of Dad's life. We threw out a printer that no longer worked, files from old patients, a soccer-coaching handbook, and a framed piece of printer paper filled with polka-dot bubble letters spelling Dr. Norris (a drawing from a young girl that Dad had once saved). We saved things too. Mom kept his old yearbooks, and my brother took his vinyl collection. In a white-and-green cardboard box, I stacked every letter of his I could find, hundreds of them. On top of these, I placed an old notebook from his college days and any lecture notes he'd written or printed. Before closing the lid, I shuffled in clear plastic sleeves of his lecture slides, two carousels filled with images, and a slide projector to view them. The lid wouldn't close properly, and I carried this box with me back to college and to graduate school and into the rest of my life.

Hyperbaric oxygen works like this: you've stepped on a nail or your swatch of skin from sternum to thighs has been sliced off or you've been cut open or a part of you cut off. Somehow, you're wounded. Your skin is gone, ripped away to reveal wet insides, jeweled flesh glistening like mounds of pulped raspberries. Your hurt is clear, and your body wants to heal itself. To fend off infection and prepare for repair, blood vessels ooze, and fluid leaks into soft tissue as nutrients and white blood cells pile up around the wound like logs cut for winter. Swelling deforms what you thought you knew of your body. Feel it push against your skin as it grapples for more room. The inflamed flesh is warm to the touch, and the swelling is so expansive, so intrusive, so pervasive, that the supply of oxygen is cut off from the wound. The tissue around the opening is suffocated. It necrotizes. It dies.

So HBO works like this: you slide into a clear chamber, a tipped bird feeder, where air pressure is increased. You feel compressed, and in fact, you are. Oxygen embraces the body and the wound, pushing in on the inflammation and squeezing it tightly. The swelling reduces, and oxygen returns to the tissue. The wound can breathe once more.

Dad's Kodak projector slides slip into the black rotary tray, and light reanimates their stories. I sit alone on the rough carpet of my living room floor and click through the carousel, through pieces of his overbleached HBO lecture, past the text and illustrations, past equations and considerations, past accepted conditions and Dalton's law, and into the human body flayed open.

This is what I want to see: the damage. It's wounds that expose life, that let us see its underpinnings. I want to look at pain made visible.

The projector whirs as it resurrects hurts. In this slide, a ruler is taped to the bottom of a foot, the blurred adhesive already falling away, refusing to stick. Bruises cloud down the center of the sole and cling to the toes' creases like charcoal rubbed from canvas. I imagine this person came down hard on something harder. Maybe they fell foot-first on a sundial or an exposed sprinkler head. In the center of the photo, an inch-wide halo of gold circumscribes the wound. The opening has a diameter of only five centimeters, but I stare into the hole filling with blood and wonder how deep it goes.

A wound: I went under screaming. I'd had trouble sleeping or, rather, had trouble breathing while sleeping. I was four years old, and my breath broke open like sores. Every night I slept in gasps, my chest rising and falling with a violence I never witnessed but felt upon waking. My rib cage ached; I needed more air.

So one morning, before breakfast, Dad flashed a penlight onto the back of my throat. I sat at the dinner table as he tilted my chin up, holding it like you might touch a statue of yourself, tenderly and with purpose. My legs swung free beneath the chair, and my fingers, unable to find a place to rest, picked at the edge of my shorts, yanked on loose strands of hair, and danced over the freckles dotting my arms. I tried to still my fidgeting body, but I was buzzing with the electricity of Dad's undivided attention. He'd be alive for thirteen more years, but already I wanted to absorb every moment with him, new gauze sopping up blood. He was freshly showered, and his damp hair smelled of Sea Breeze shampoo. "Say ahhhh," he said, and I did. I watched from my tipped head as he looked inside my mouth, reading my body. He squinted, then clicked off the light.

He found inflamed tonsils, two too-large orbs blocking my airway. My adenoids were too big, too, and the opening at the back of my throat was the size of a pencil. Dad wanted to help me breathe, and he knew what to do. I ended up in a scratchy hospital bed with my back exposed when I sat up. My white underwear peeked through the backless gown, and while I wasn't old enough to be embarrassed, the open dress still bothered me. Cold air shimmied down my spine, and I shivered. Dad held my hand.

I'd never needed anesthesia before because I'd never needed surgery. I was four years old, and I'd been healthy—lucky. Initially, because Dad was a doctor, the surgeons said he could stay with me until I went to sleep, but the doors to the operating room swung open, and he was kept on one side as I was pushed to the other. I screamed and kept screaming till I blacked out. My shrieks were high pitched and piercing. They cut through everything else. Time ripped open, and there was only one sharp sound. When I woke, I had no memory of my screams, but Mom never forgot them, the way my lungs screeched when they took my dad away from me.

The paper clip rusted onto Dad's lecture notes, leaving oxidized trails like veins. I pinch the pages and turn them with care, as though they might disintegrate at any moment. The paper is thin and yellowed, and it smells exactly how you think it would smell. I read through his notes on "Historical Perspective" and try to compute the "Basic Physiology." On the third page, I linger on the first of HBO's three mechanisms of action: hyperoxygenation.

On a fat boxy computer, Dad typed, "Normally the hemoglobin molecule carries 97.5% (or 19.5 volume-percent) of the oxygen in blood while the plasma carries 2.5% or 0.5 volume percent. Tissues extract approximately 5.0 volume percent of oxygen to meet baseline requirements. At 2 ATA the plasma carries 2.3 volume percent and at 3 ATA the plasma carries 6.9 volume percent—enough to sustain life."

Let's break it down: ATA stands for atmospheres absolute and acts as a measurement of pressure in HBO therapy. It quantifies the pressure necessary to revive wounds. If you want a wound to breathe again, if you don't want a part of your body to die, you've got to push down on it. One ATA is equal to the weight of air at sea level. On any beach, at any edge, the pressure is the same: one ATA. Descending thirty-three feet into seawater doubles the weight, and descending thirty-three more, sixty-six feet, so deep that in clouded waters, the sun must work to crack through, triples the pressure. At three ATA, your blood's plasma carries more than ten times the oxygen it can normally bear; it's enough oxygen to keep you alive through blood loss. In HBO, three ATA, a deep dark sea, is the heaviest weight used to keep a wound alive.

Nestled beside my reading chair, Dad's box sleeps in the corner. I moved to the Southwest five years after he died, for grad school, and in this dry heat and this dry land, no one else knows him. Every day, after teaching or hiking or drinking beer on friends' porches, I come home to his slides and notes and letters. After setting down my things, my canvas bag heavy with books or the better half of a six-pack, I sit down, bundle myself in a blanket, and read his writing not meant for me.

These words were once his, and this box is all I have left. I feel the weight of it. His research notebook from college field studies (titled "The Origin of the Feces") presses up against his outstanding faculty award (an engraved black plaque on dark wood) presses up against an elementary school report card (mostly A's but B's in social studies, conduct, and writing). They all sit together, these dated layers of his life shuffled into a reused cardboard box marked "Pool Stuff."

Above the box, I hung two photos. In 1985, Dad went to Alaska on OB/GYN rotation, helping to birth over thirty babies in the bright chunk of a rural hospital he called "the yellow submarine." He was twenty-four that summer, the same age I was when I first put up these photos. In the top picture, red suspenders tug his rubber waders up and match his knit cap (complete with a white pompom). He holds a bludgeoning stone in one hand while the other hooks a dead salmon through its open mouth and gills, a loose suture coming undone. Beside him, his friend holds two branches they've jerry-rigged into a Y formation, a net woven between the two arms of the tree-like letter. Beneath this photo hangs another: beside two light blue kayaks, Dad and his friend pose at the water's edge of a stone-filled beach, curling their arms to show off the little muscle they've acquired. When the camera's timer clicked off, I imagine they collapsed in laughter. How ridiculous, these two skinny boys pretending to be tough.

Before I hung these photos, I neglected to check the wall for studs, just placed the silver nail against paint and hammered. I hit cinderblock. And I hit cinderblock. And I hit cinderblock. I cried in frustration—I couldn't even memorialize him properly—but continued until I got the nail to stick. Now, when I look at the bottom photo, at my dad strong-manning with his friend, I remember that, behind it, pressed against it, two holes bleed dust onto the floor.

I project each slide onto my living room wall, the sound of the machine's fan and the click of slides my only companion as I spend time in each wound. In this image, the stomach skin has been peeled off in one quick curl. Marbled muscle and off-white fat streak through like smudges on a chalkboard. Through the sticky pink of an exposed body, blood vessels thin and pool. Brown tributaries trend toward the tips of the thighs, and I wonder: what happened to this person? The cut most likely made way for a skin graft, but there's no written reason for why one was necessary. The black blurring the skin's wet edges suggests a bad burn. But how was this person burned? Who left them alone with a giant flame? Who left them alone?

Dad's slides don't show faces, only injuries. A ruler is laid on top of the peninsula of skin that reaches down from one but-terflied rib toward the promise of leg. Its clean edges attempt to measure the gnarled hurt, but this ruler is useless—it can't measure even half the damage.

Wounds can tell us a lot about a person, but most of their qualities aren't quantifiable. Length, width, depth, sure, but what number can depict the careful way a patient holds their burned arm to the camera? What equation can capture the way a shoulder curls inward ashamed of its gash? What data-set can describe the way the wound's hungry mouth transmits its howl to me? The only way to know these people is through their wounds, so I study them.

I live alone. I keep the box of Dad's things in the corner of my room, but I never show it to anyone. Sometimes friends will eye it when they come over for dinner or tea, but they never ask, and I never offer. When we're chatting or eating or doing both, I sit across from them and across from the box, keeping my eyes on it and theirs from it. I'm protective of it in a way I don't know how to explain. What would I say? It's impossible to understand losing a parent at a young age without losing a parent at a young age. It's impossible to know my dad with-out knowing my dad. I don't talk about him, don't tell doctors my full family history, don't chitchat with the dentist about which parent I'm closest to, don't correct strangers when they ask where my parents live, don't tell that boy he wore Converse high tops too, don't tell lovers how he cooked pancakes with faces, don't tell friends he used to order Honeybell oranges for the juiciest citrus, don't tell myself how much I miss him.

I used to try to bring him up in conversations, but I was met with stories about funerals for distant relations or I was met with pitying looks from people who "couldn't imagine" or I was met with nothing. Blank stares. Silence. It's just another way Dad has been taken from me. Now, I keep the pain to myself. When his name rises in my throat, I hear others in my head: Shouldn't I get over it already? It's been seven years. What do I want people to say? What is there to say?

All the toes are flooded with blood, the toenails wiped clean. Along the top of the foot, red outlines the gashes, but the fat of the foot glistens yellow. At the ankle, two safety pins poke into the pain of opened skin. In the next slide, the arch of the foot is slashed open. And in the next, there's healing, the result of HBO, skin reaching to hold itself. But I don't look at the healing slides; I fall into the wounds. They draw me in, a magnet pulling metal, like matching up to like. Over the years, I've been told I cry too much, that my writing is a "maudlin plea," that I'm too sad to be friends with. Sometimes I wish I were different, but we can't change the shape the hot metal core of us cooled into being.

In my darkened apartment, I pour myself into these slides. These photos show an extreme case of diabetic foot ulcers. Excess glucose can damage nerves, causing numbness in feet, masking what would be pain. This numbness is a problem because pain is vital for survival.

After breaking in new shoes or going for a long walk or standing more often than not, a patient might remove their shoes, unlace each tennis shoe, pull one aglet, then the other, tug the shoe off heel by dirt-caked heel, then roll the sock down, pinch the cloth toe, and pull. After the ritual process of unsheathing the foot, the patient may find: blood, bones, irreparable damage.

❦

I watch fish swim through a tank, their silver and green and yellow scales slicing through the water like knives cutting through dry sand. The room is dark and cool, and I let children and retirees filter through in front of me. They press their hands against the glass, point to the biggest fish, then toddle off, but I stand fixed at the back. I look past their constant movement and settle into the rhythmic burble of water.

I come to the aquarium often, and often alone, because the fish remind me of Dad. Before he became a doctor, he considered becoming a marine biologist, and in one of his old notebooks, I found pen sketches of striped sergeant majors, spotted rock beauties, and wide southern stingrays. I imagine his hand, steady and quick, pushing the ballpoint tip against an expanse of notebook paper. In the tank, I look for the same fish.

I'm liable to cry watching these creatures, so I come alone because I don't want to explain why to someone who came with me only hoping to coo at jellyfish. It's not that I don't want to talk about him; it's that other people don't want to listen. When someone laughs at the thick glasses their father wears and I mention my dad wore glasses too, there is silence. When I'm sharing a piece of key lime pie and note that it was my dad's favorite, the only response is an eked out "Mmm." When we pass a hospital and I explain why I shudder, the car whines down the highway, and I listen to the wind whistle past. Most people don't like to think about pain, but I can't stop prodding it.

Under the blue aquarium lights, the fish loop around each other, threading over and under tender bellies and scything fins. They swoop around the algae rocks, searching for an end to the tank's edges. As I watch these sea creatures circling and circling, swimming faster and slower, eyes anchored to one image or flitting around the water, I feel the weight of the years on my chest: the missed birthdays, the missed graduations, the visits home to a half-empty house. Every flash of fin jolts my heart and makes me think, "I wish Dad was here." The heaviness pushes in on my sternum, and I wonder how the thing that hurts me is the thing that keeps me breathing.

When I've neglected my grief too long, when I've spent days without mentioning his favorite beer (Blue Moon), the sound of his voice (scratchy and melodic), how his hands felt (warm), I flip the blinds closed, click off my phone, and pull his box from the corner of my room to sift through its contents: the hundreds of letters, the dozens of newspaper clippings, the tens of photos. I dive into his HBO lecture and shrug off numbness like a peel of sunburned skin.

With a can of sparkling water in one hand, I read about HBO's second mechanism of action, bubble reduction. As air pushes down on the body, it shrinks any bubbles caught in the blood. As these bubbles decrease in size, O's shrinking to o's, their surface tension increases, and, as my dad writes, "the bubble becomes unstable and finally collapses." I sip from the can, and the liquid shimmers down my throat. This is a lecture I've read often, one that I keep circling back to, one that echoes around in my skull as I'm walking to class, to dinner, and back home again. These wounds, their care, won't leave me. After a while, the words swell in my brain, blocking out everything else. When the pressure becomes too much, I shut myself indoors. For hours, my gate flexes locked, my curtains hang closed, and I cocoon myself within, a skeleton covered over with muscle and skin. Often, I don't realize I haven't left the house until my stomach grumbles.

Under the seeping sunset, I walk down the street for a three-dollar slice of big pizza and come back home to eat it, letting the grease drip down my hands as I continue reading. There's no one to talk to about my dad, so I read alone in my tiny casita. His bigness overfills the four-hundred-square-foot space, present in the pictures, the pages, the wall, the air. I keep reading his lecture and let it take me over. Next up, HBO's third mechanism of action: desiccation. Dad writes, "This effect follows the lack of water vapor in 100% O_2. It has no clinical application and can actually adversely affect wound healing by its drying action."

Dry dressing wounds in thin gauze used to be a wound-healing norm, but in truth, a wound should be kept wet for healing. To re-form the skin that's been scuffed off, cells migrate up within the wound, slinking from hair follicle and sweat gland ducts, while other cells migrate over from the skin at the wound's edges, a lakeshore expanding.

This was discovered in 1962, when a silver scalpel flicked twelve wounds onto the backs of young pigs. These wounds were two and a half centimeters wide and one hundredth to three hundredths of a centimeter deep, which meant they were classified as superficial, not deep enough to warrant concern. Still, I wonder if these animals felt the pain of their cuts, if years later, these pigs might remember what it felt like to be sliced open.

Thin polythene film covered half the wounds; the others were left alone. The six uncovered wounds dried and formed scabs, natural bandages to hide the depth of the lesion, a protection and an impediment. As new skin cells migrated up and in, some crusted into scabs and hardened into ugly hurt, delaying true healing. The wet wounds, though, the ones tended to and cared for, the ones kept open and fresh, bloody and alive, healed twice as fast.

Mom kept Dad's ashes in her closet for a year, greeting them each day as she undressed and redressed herself. The urn was a blue box with half crescents pushed in on the ends. It sat on top of a crate filled with Dad's winter sweaters, at eye level, looking back at her as she slipped on her pink velvet pajamas or her weathered Virginia sweatshirt or her pantsuit with creases pressed crisp down each leg. It was there when she came home from basketball games, work, or dinner with friends. The thick paper holding Dad's ashes was handmade, and bits of hardness ran through the smooth night-blue like ribs poking through a flimsy lung.

On the first anniversary of his death, she buckled the urn into the car and drove toward the ocean. We paddled red kayaks over plough mud and around islands of long-toothed grass. The sun sat heavy on my shoulders and humidity hung like cobwebs—the weight felt unbearable. The paddles slung into the water, and with each shoulder rotation, small ripples ran toward the shore. We kept going until we couldn't. Mom said something, though I don't remember what, and then she placed the biodegradable urn in the water. It didn't dissolve right away but cradled through the ocean, swinging side to side as it descended, bubbles leaking out as Dad sunk deeper and deeper and out of sight. As water became memorial, I dipped one hand in the sea. The warm salt licked the lines of my palm.

Here is what I remember: he didn't like goat cheese; he liked Talking Heads. We made blueberry muffins together. He was a strong swimmer. He ran Thursday afternoons with Mike, an artist, and Dell, a former marine. Once, toward the end but before I knew the end was coming, I asked if he wanted to go running. He took the stairs two steps at a time and came back with his sneakers in hand. We ran past camellias and under dogwood trees. Tree roots pressed up under the sidewalk, and the concrete cracked in half like hands reaching for prayer. I ran quickly because I wanted to know how much my body could take. Before long, my hair slicked itself to my neck, and my lungs ached for oxygen.

☙❧

In this slide, the patient holds the ruler in their hand, but the camera's flash bleaches out the numbers. It's a useless tool for gauging the healing progress of an amputation. I don't know why this patient needed half of their leg cut off, but I know there's only so much we can save of one another. The leg opens at the knee, a toothless mouth, gums yellow and pink and howling. What must it have felt like? Like a steak hitting a hot pan, like a weed ripped from the ground, like a body losing itself.

This is the third slide in the patient's healing series, the other two are close-up captures of the open wound, so close the surrounding anatomy is lost: there's the wound and skin but no markers of the human surrounding the pain. In this slide, though, the camera moves out to see the thigh pulled open, thin hands pursed together, elbows pressed into blankets, a dotted hospital gown rumpled at the neck, the thin corner of a mouth hovering at the frame's edge. This image is harder for me to look at because I can see the pain in context, but I force myself to study it, to see hurt growing in a human body. As Susan Sontag says in *Regarding the Pain of Others*, "There is the satisfaction of being able to look at the image without flinching. There is the pleasure of flinching." I don't know if it's healthy, me spending all this time looking at wounds, but it feels better than looking away.

☙❧

When I ran in the South, leaping over cracked sidewalks, spotted sunlight trickling through trees, the scent of jasmine and barbecue hanging in humidity, I ran the same route Dad and I did, taking the same turns, the same hill, the same straightaway home. Sweat stuck to my body, ran into my eyes, slipped over my nose and climbed into my mouth. The sweat stayed with me. The air was already too heavy; it couldn't carry anything else.

In the Southwest, where I live now, I have to run farther, run longer, add miles to miles to keep the sweat from evaporating. I run till my legs quiver, and my lungs quiver, and my body weighs itself down with wetness. At the end of the run, I know that this is what Dad felt—the distance overcome, yes, but also, mostly, his body, in this place, alive.

Dive into deep water, past the point of filtered sun and into the darkest depths. Down there, wetsuits cling to skin, hoarding any heat that remains. Fish pierce the darkness, and bubbles break toward breakage. Time bends; light shatters; the world is unmade. If you hold your breath too long or swim toward the sun too fast, when you rupture the water's surface, you'll feel a small pop within you. It sounds satisfying, a slight release inside your body, a valve allowed to breathe, but it could kill you, coming up for air too quickly.

Alveoli, the air sacs in your lungs shaped like a bundle of fish eggs, can rupture when scuba diving. When these air sacs burst, their escaped air can migrate into arteries, blocking the flow of blood. This bubble of air can glide into the brain, the heart, the lungs and result in death. The potentially fatal damage hides inside you, invisible to the outside world. To treat an arterial air embolism, you need to sink onto the tongue of an HBO chamber, let it shrink the bubble, crinkle the air so that the blood can move around it, so that the blood can hold the hurt.

Once, when I was in elementary school, I spent the day with Dad at work. We crisscrossed through the hospital's hallways, and he introduced me to other doctors, nurses, administrators, and to his closest co-worker confidant, a woman with a big laugh who would reintroduce herself to me a decade later at his memorial service. I don't remember her name, but I remember she was kind. When he needed to see patients, I sat in his office, trying to teach myself to juggle weighted balls painted like globes. I could never keep all the balls in the air at once; one, inevitably, splatted on the ground.

Dad had worked at the same hospital for years, but this was the first time I'd visited him. Even then, it felt like a gift, an offer to see his world outside of me. All day, we walked around the hospital, threading through half-empty rooms, picking up rubber gloves to blow into chicken-comb balloons. After lunch, we wandered into the wound-healing center, where he began talking to another doctor, where he looked at a chart, where he did something to heal someone without me. I lay on the outstretched tongue of an HBO chamber and watched him in his white coat, his glasses secured behind his ears with a neon-green knit cord. His back was turned to me, but I watched his index finger scan through a patient's chart. As I watched him, one of Dad's future pallbearers slid the chamber's tongue in. I was swallowed by the tube, a piglet without blood. I touched the clear wall separating me from my dad, and I screamed. I'm still screaming.

WISH YOU WERE HERE

he first postcard depicts an old couple, an elderly man and woman holding each other close, foreheads touching, image cut close to show only part of their faces, centering the diamond of space opened between their heads and chests. Next, zoomed further out, a mad-scientist type with a thick mustache and round glasses grips a chair, his suit jacket a half size too big. The third: a young child, younger than two, rests his head on his knuckles, thinking. His head looks too big for his body (it takes up almost the full frame), and his thick mat of hair doesn't match his sleek, naked abdomen. I can't tell if the picture was altered or if I don't understand age. Perhaps both. The final photo is out of focus or focusing on something unseen. Two fuzzy women, their mouths below the frame, whisper to each other, one's hand cupped to the other's ear. A secret held between the two.

These four postcards are taped to the window frames in my childhood bedroom. They aren't the only ones—dozens of postcards outline my windows with smaller windows to elsewhere. A sailboat from Harbor Island and a Dutch pond spotted with swans sandwich one of Van Gogh's self-portraits. The Malmö cityscape sits above the Coliseum, which sits above the Sistine

Chapel. Most of the images are of places or art; they're cards I plucked from a tourist-trap stand to stand in for a memory that would inevitably fade, leaving only the postcard as residue. But the four black-and-white postcards, the ones clustered together on the right side of the room, the couple, the man, the child, and the women, these are different.

When my dad died, these four images began to haunt me. I don't mean that I saw them in everything, that I thought about them every day. I didn't; I don't. But when I thought of these images, when some phrase or tilt of the head conjured these four postcards, I fell out of the room, out of time and space. They denatured the present, light burning holes through film, and I couldn't grasp why, not entirely.

I don't remember exactly how I got them, but I can recreate the memory through the scraps of what I know, what I have. As a teenager, I must have been laying the other postcards on my bed, arranging them horizontally before lifting them vertically. I might've held one of the dark wooden posts to my canopy bed, or perhaps I stood on my polka-dotted comforter, towering above the images as the sun melted into my mint-green walls. Maybe I was taping some of them up, putting Picasso's clown and the Statue of Liberty on opposite sides, deciding where Long Creek Falls should go, the aquarium's emperor penguins, Body Worlds. Where does this memory touch another? I was mapping the anatomy of time, and in the midst of this, Dad must have knocked, poking his Roman nose into my room, the four glossy images clutched in his hand, my future ghosts. He must have looked at me, eyes shining behind wire-rimmed glasses, and asked, "Would you like these?"

People point to different beginnings for the postcard. The true beginning depends on what you classify as a postcard. Does it need a picture? A stamp? A sender and recipient? Historically, the earliest origin suggested is 1840, when the practical jokester Theodore Hook hand-painted a small card with caricatured post-office clerks sporting big foreheads and big noses, a joke meant to rankle the postal workers who would handle the note. It was a prank not unlike one Dad would've pulled. Hook mailed the card to himself sans written message, and many see this as the first postcard, but, because the card wasn't sent for communication between two people, I don't see it as the true beginning of postcards, only one of the guideposts pointing toward the starting line.

Twenty-five years later, another guidepost. At the Austro-German Postal Conference, Prussian postal official Dr. Heinrich von Stephan proposed "an open post-sheet" with one side devoted to an address and the other devoted to a message, but the idea was quickly rejected due to privacy concerns. Who would want their message meant for one open for many? Four years after this initial pitch, a similar proposal was accepted, but no images were suggested or included. An address on one side, and a message on the other, but what of the image?

For me, then, postcards began in 1870, in France, at Camp Conlie, under dire conditions. The camp was founded during the Franco-Prussian War to train new recruits. Eighty thousand men were sent there, but when they arrived, no housing had been built, so they slept in emergency tents under poor conditions with little access to weaponry.

Picture this: the ground is damp, muddy. It's difficult to walk through. Boots suction to the earth. Every hour is a physical slog. Every day is cold. In the morning, you wake up cold, frost on the ground. During the day, you're grateful for any light that can penetrate the gray skies, but at night, there's no chance of a respite. You go to bed cold. Even crammed next to other bodies, arm against arm, one breath bleeding into another, you shiver. Shouldn't you be sweating, overheating? So close to someone, yet your body closes up. Disease runs rampant. Every week, someone else's skin bubbles over with blisters. Smallpox takes ten, twenty, fifty-plus men. You feel alone. The only comfort is a letter home, a thin tether between here and someplace warmer, some face warmer.

So, in 1870, the men wrote home. They covered blank pages with their hopes, fears, and longings. Léon Besnardeau, a bookseller who worked close to the camp, quickly ran out of paper. When he'd sold all the paper in his notebooks, he cut their covers into rectangles and sold them too. When he ran out of covers, he printed blank cards. A banner rippled across the top: "Souvenir de la Défense Nationale" (souvenir meaning remembrance, memory). Below the banner, three open lines were wreathed with greenery, and around the greenery ran another ribbon: "famille," "honneur," "patrie," and "liberté" twined around the leaves. In this card, Theodore Hook's imagery met with Dr. Heinrich von Stephan's messages and the first postcard, as I see it, was sent. Postcards, then, were born out of desperation. An urgent need to tell another about where you are, how you are, who.

I sift through the box of letters my dad wrote to my grandmother, the ones she must have read through after he died, the ones I inherited from her when she died. While he was away at school, he wrote and sent hundreds of notes home. Most are mundane glimpses into his day: studying for bio, listening to Dizzy, making dinner with friends. His concerns seemed small; he wrote simply to feel close to his family (and ask for money for books and winter tires). There is nothing extraordinary about his letters except that they capture a time I have no other entrance to. It would be a decade before I was born, and yet these letters let me slip into the stream of my dad's days before he was my dad, when he was young, hurrying toward the rest of his life, wondering what it would hold.

What is extraordinary is that these letters make time travel possible. They keep small moments of Dad's day in amber. I can hold the past in my hand, look into it and see movement suspended in place, a bug in the midst of flapping its wings long after its last breath. I see the library, the windows frosted with winter air. I see the kitchen, a pot of pasta on the brim of boiling over. The dorm room, the desk, the postcard waiting to be written. His notes are brief records of what happened just before and what will come immediately after—I feel the contained motion within them.

Postcards capture only a moment, but they do it well. Dad gave me the four blank black-and-white postcards, but they came from a larger collection he'd had for years. In the box of his letters, I find dozens of these monochrome cards, the back of each one crystallizing a singular split second of his life. Maybe this is why Dad's black-and-white postcards are so absorbing to me: they are snapshots, preserved milliseconds. They mimic the messages scrawled on their backs. On the front of one a young boy in Sicily stands bundled in a sweater that makes his jacket too tight; the fabric pulls at his single front button, and the shoulder stitches stretch against his scapulas. He wears a newsboy cap and grins. It's as if he was running, paused for the picture, and is eager to be running again. On the back of the card, in my dad's small, boxy handwriting, "Today I get my locks shorn." I remember this: when he was in college, his father, a military man, sent him enough money to get his hair cut weekly, but Dad would save the money and go to the barber only once or twice a year. He writes that he has five tests, three finals, two projects, and four labs coming up, but this weekend is Green Key weekend, so he'll "play some work some too." Even with no way of knowing, I'm sure he finished all his work before he did any playing; he had a dedicated work ethic, one that he passed down to me. He was regimented, some would say strict to a fault, but the truth is that structure is now how I get through my days. It's how I survive. Dad signs off, "Got to go to class. Take care." In these postcards, he is perpetually going to class, dashing off a postcard, sending his love, living his daily life. In these postcards, he is perpetually alive.

～～～～～～

There's no question: I take after my dad. We laughed at the same jokes, loved the same books, were fascinated by the same things. We could spend hours walking around the neighborhood in the early evening, talking about nothing in particular, old Green Day, Fulham FC, what I learned in school that day. We chatted as we wandered beneath blooming dogwoods and big oak trees, often stopping for ice cream on the way home once the sun sank below the horizon. We filled our days with each other's company. We just liked spending time together.

Someone suggested, in edits, that I show my dad's faults to make him more real to readers, but I don't know that he had any other than the ones all humans do: that we are fragile creatures who love well and die. Perhaps I was too young to recognize his faults, but he was, to me, even at the time, a faultless father. He loved me well, and he did his best and saw me as I was and loved me for that. I don't know what more I could have asked for except time.

When he died, time broke into before and after. Before, I collected postcards, but I never wrote on them. I'd never been separated from someone I wanted to share my life with. He'd been there for these moments. We ate shrimp burgers at that beach and rode our bikes past those red tulips and paddled down that rushing river in helmets and life vests. These images constellated our collective memories. There was no need to caption them for one another because we'd lived them together.

After, it was like I stepped into a house of mirrors: everywhere I turned, whether I was in North Carolina, Arizona, or Prague, there was only me, alone. I stopped collecting postcards. Everywhere was the same. Forests, deserts, beaches.

Cold, hot, sunny, rainy. Everything was the same: empty. I was unanchored, unmoored. Time passed through me. I left the place where I grew up because it felt wrong to be there without him. Of course, it felt wrong to be anywhere without him. I went to college and graduate school in cities where no one else knew my dad. No one wanted to hear about my grief. The only thing that stopped the spinning, that collapsed the distance, was his box of letters. To cut open the daze, I would take out a single postcard, read the words he wrote when he was my age, and rub the paper to remind myself that these memories were real, that I couldn't touch him, but I could touch what remained. It wasn't enough, but it's what I had.

Before the First World War, roughly one million seven hundred thousand letters were sent through the mail every day. When the war started, that number jumped. Each day, civilians sent between three and four million letters to the frontline, and soldiers wrote approximately two million back. That's three million three hundred thousand more pieces of paper sent through the post each day. Stacked up, that's roughly two Washington Monuments of paper, almost four Statues of Liberty. Mail sacks overflowed with these notes, letters upon letters pressed against each other like geological layers of daily correspondence, many of which were postcards.

It took three days for a card to travel from the frontline to behind the lines, and three days for one to travel back. Six days. During wartime, every second is vital, every one could be the last, so time is stretched out, pulled open into cirrus clouds. Six days is a long time during war, too long, so many soldiers wrote daily, sometimes more than that. In the muddy trenches, between the bursts of fire, they pulled out their pens and pencils. Their letters were censored, of course: they couldn't comment on their precise location, their next moves, troop morale, or the number of deaths. What they could say: I'm alive. A postcard's combination of message and photo communicated as much as the sender could in as little time as possible.

On the home front, families waited for the mail, and when it came, they dutifully wrote back. What more could they do? Mostly they wrote trivial things, not wanting to overburden the soldiers with their own difficulties. Here is what we are having for dinner, and here is what the neighbor said, and your sister scraped her knee today. The writing kept the soldiers connected to their home life, their old life. It said: this is waiting for you; we've kept it warm.

Of course, not all soldiers had families. So, in 1915, a system of marraines de guerre, or wartime godmothers, was created. These women signed up to write to isolated soldiers with the hopes of keeping up their morale. They were matched up randomly, by need. This soldier needs someone, and you can be that person. They wrote back and forth, strangers sharing their daily lives with one another in the hopes of surviving. Because here is what it boils down to: this connection, these postcards, the idea that you were tied to someone else, that you were needed, that you were cared for, was a reach toward life.

It's been seven years. Postcards preserve time, but they can't stop it. I can't send Dad a postcard now. How would I address it? I could write to someone else, but who would I send it to? I write letters to friends and family, sure, but there's a casual intimacy in the dailiness of postcards that I can't break through. Because of the postcard's clipped format, the recipient must necessarily understand the framework of the writer's life, and I don't know how to shorthand my days for someone I won't let in it, not entirely. I'm terrified of more loss.

So instead of writing, each time I go home, I visit my postcards.

I always commune alone. I climb the stairs and take a left in the hallway, round the same corners I used to when my parents told me it was bedtime. I turn my bedroom's glass door-knob and push. In the winter, the door sticks and squeals open after a little shove, but in the summer, it yields with no resis-tance. I stand in the doorway and look at my postcards, taking in the whole of them from afar before stepping closer, studying a specific one, running my finger over its face and falling into it. I talk myself through my life.

See that coastline dotted with yachts and expensive cars? We took pictures pretending we fit in as we walked to the aquarium where we'd follow fish with our fingers and watch jellyfish float in a dark room under ultraviolet lights.

And at that amusement park, we ate swirled soft serve that melted in the heat. Dad showed me the ride he used to work, the lazy river. When he was teenager, he got so bored as a life-guard that he'd tell guests to "take all children firmly by the hair." Almost no one noticed, but he amused himself.

Oh, and we rode rented bikes past that silo and over that bridge. I'd forgotten this: how no one else wore helmets, so lo-cals sometimes stopped and pointed, marveling at us as we wheeled by. We were foreign images to look at. I was teetering on the edge of adolescence and incredibly embarrassed, but I knew better than to ask Dad if I could ride without my helmet. He would do anything to protect me.

I move through my room as I would an art exhibit, lingering on any image that draws me in before sidling to the next. Inev-itably, I settle on the four black-and-white postcards, the ones he gave me. They're clustered together on the right side of my room, vining down a window frame. Maybe it's the mystery of them that brings me back. These faces are different than the landscapes I collected. They keep secrets from me. The memo-ries held within aren't mine; they're Dad's, and his life doesn't swing open when I look at them. Maybe these postcards re-minded him of some store, some friend, or simply a time in his life when he used to write postcards; I don't know. As much as I study the old woman's ring and the scientist's glasses, the girl's fingernails and the baby's creases, I can't know. They catalogue a time long gone, and while so much remains elusive, I'm grateful to have these small windows to the unknown. A map to territory I can't reach. Proof that something more exists.

❦

Most deltiologists ("deltos" as in writing or tablet, "-logist" as in one who studies, "deltiologist" as in postcard collector) have a niche: a time period, a place, an artist. They collect postcards of kilts, Pennsylvania, and Main Streets across the States. Vintage cars, tattoos, and art deco hotels. Parrots, propaganda, and superlatives (the biggest, the smallest, the worst, the best).

Whatever it is they collect, they archive history with their postcards. If you look through Diane McKenzie's hospital postcard collection, for example, you can see the buildings accordion out, including the one where my dad first saw his cancer. The small houses and elegant estates disappear, replaced by rectangular constructions with immaculate windows like the ones I know so well. This collection, like all collections, moves you through the story of a thing. Collections answer questions like: What did this look like? How did it change? What is it people want to remember? The still frames of individual cards add up to something larger than themselves. Like movie frames flipped through, movement emerges through accumulation and conservation. Stalled time starts to move. A story outlines itself.

I didn't set out to collect postcards, but the impulse to buy them felt automatic. I bought one postcard, and then another, and later, another. Looking back, I suppose it was the ease of them, the way they compacted memory to a small piece of paper that could be picked up and remembered, but at the time, I didn't think about why I bought them. I simply accrued the cards without thought, keeping them in different drawers, on my desk, and stuck in the frame of my bathroom mirror. When it came time to leave a place I loved, I found myself in gift shops and airports and makeshift pop-up shops fingering the edge of an image. I don't know when they stopped being disparate objects and became a collection, but eventually, the number of cards piling up made the transition undeniable. I had, unwittingly, created an archive of my life. It was the story I wanted to tell myself about where I'd been, where I was going, who I was, and who I was with.

I wasn't the first collector, of course; the human history of collecting stretches back to our beginnings as hunter-gatherers. Our ancestors' frontal lobes, like ours, integrated information about value and memory. They knew to store food for harsh winters because they'd experienced scarce food supplies in the past. When they moved, they took useful tools with them, sensing that they may need them in the future. They compared the past to the present and projected into the future. These impulses helped them survive, so the genes that precipitated collecting passed through generations, and they remain in us today. In thinking about time, we are always thinking about death. Physical survival looks different now, sure, fewer bears and more heart disease, but the old tools still apply to emotional survival. We survive as we always have—by moving through time.

Our collections, like those of our ancestors', contain time. Perhaps we collect toy cars, like the ones we loved in childhood, each Hot Wheel transporting us into our beloved past. Or maybe we collect expensive art, which can harness our emotions too, but also acts as a financial investment for the future. Or maybe we collect for the pure pleasure of sharing our collection with someone else. I think about my postcard collection, or rather, my postcard collections, plural, both mine and my dad's, the ones I bought and the ones he sent. I think of what it means to alight upon a familiar place in his and to place him within mine. *I, too, remember this place, this bridge pictured, this ruin captured.* Memories become entwined, coagulating in each collection. It sounds like a cheesy T-shirt slogan, the kind you'd find in a beach-front store with keychains and shot glasses, but it's also true: collections create connections.

The cardinal's nest in the tree by the garage, the creaks the AC makes at night, the warmth of the dog lying on me. I think about the postcards I would send Dad now, what I would say, what I need to tell him. How the white jasmine is blooming, the smell of garbage on my walks, the new jacket I bought. I think about what he is missing: my life. What moments could I save to share with him, only him? The way pasta dough feels when stretched thin, the smell of my T-shirt after a long run, the taste of a peach not yet ripe. I can never seem to wait for peaches to ripen; my sense of timing is all off.

Five years after I stopped collecting postcards, I taught a group of undergrads about mapping. One day, we sat outside, redrawing the world around us, and after class, a student lingered and asked if we could talk. She often looked out the window during class, then tuned back in to offer an insightful comment before twisting to watch the sky once more. That day, after class, we sat on a stone bench in the sun, and she hunched her back, rifling through her bag as she told me about a community meeting on gentrification. She looked up and smiled as she pulled a postcard from her bag. It was an artist's rendering of downtown, and she handed it to me. It was the first postcard I'd acquired after Dad died, one that depicted my new home. I remembered the marraines de guerre, those wartime godmothers who wrote to strangers to keep them alive, and I smiled back.

Later that year, Mom and I went to Seattle to look at whales and visit one of Dad's old friends. One afternoon, we walked downhill from our hotel toward the oldest skyscraper in the city, but we didn't realize we'd have to pay for the view. Mom and I found this ridiculous, this commodification of the sky, but we paid anyway. We wanted to see the city from above. In the lobby-turned-gift-shop, the man behind the register handed us a receipt and, paper-clipped to its back, a complimentary postcard. In it, it's night, and a cable car rolls down a cobblestone street toward the partially lit-up tower, the biggest thing in the city. It was the second postcard that found its way to me, and it became clear to me then: I'd started a new collection.

These postcards came to me by chance; they were a gifted magic, the threads of time, and I kept them in pristine condition, out of the sun and free of dust, but each time I looked at them, something built in me. I remembered my quartet of black-and-white postcards. The couple, the man, the child, the women. The way they tethered me to Dad. It's one thing to be given a postcard, but it's something else to seek one out. I mean it takes courage to look for something you might never find. There's meaning not just in the object but also in the dedication to its pursuit. There is love in looking.

It wasn't until over a year later, on Dad's birthday, when I flew across the country to go to a soccer game with Mom, that I found what I'd been looking for. He would've been fifty-nine.

That summer, the U.S. women's national team was on their victory tour after a World Cup win. Mom and I had watched them obsessively that summer, planning our days around matches. Dad played soccer growing up, and he coached my brother and me when we were young. As we got older, he came to every game, cheering from the stands. For his fiftieth birthday, we went to England for the weekend just to watch his favorite team play, an extravagant and sentimental celebration. In high school, I practiced shooting against the garage door, and when I broke a window, he ferried me to the hardware store, where we bought plexiglass so I couldn't break it again. He was so proud of me, my dedication and skill, the way I refused to see the breakability of the world.

Seven years after he died, Mom and I arrived at the game hours early. We walked around outside the stadium, stopping by the canvas tents, taking pictures with trophies, playing games to win free scarves. It was hot, and we sipped water as we circled the stadium. The air smelled of sweat and soft pretzels. Finally, I decided it was time to join the line. My favorite player sat under a white tent, taking pictures with fans and signing picture postcards. It was a player Dad had watched and admired too. She was a forward back then, back before, but had moved to defense since. Still, she was out there, on the field, even though her position had changed. Mom and I bounced on our feet as we neared the front of the line. My hands were sweaty, and I didn't know what to say. When I got to the front and squatted to take a picture, I blurted out that we had gone to the same college. I didn't tell her that I'd watched her with my dad, that today was his birthday, that my love of soccer grew from him, that I missed him every second of every day. She signed the postcard in red permanent marker and handed it to me. I blew on the ink, not wanting it to smear.

It was the first postcard I sought out, and I knew what I was doing, what it meant. I was starting a new collection, but I wasn't letting go, moving on, adhering to any hackneyed grief platitudes. I was collapsing time: in my new collection, my new home in Arizona sits beside an old skyscraper in Seattle, which sits beside a player who'd played through the decades, one Dad watched with me and I now watch without him. Time accordions itself, the past pressing against the present and reaching toward the future. I imagine showing Dad these postcards, pointing out where I live on the map, telling him about the swift breeze on the tower's ledge, that shot from outside the eighteen-yard box. I can't show him these postcards, of course not. I can't invite him to visit me, or meet me in Seattle, or call him after the championship game. I can't tell him these stories because these postcards don't bring him back. No, they can't bring him back, but they remind me of a time when I could share these moments with him. These postcards don't bring him back, no, but they bring me back to him.

DEAR HILDA

Dear Hilda,

You came to Dad's funeral, but you didn't introduce yourself. You must have shuffled among the bodies of people you didn't know, nudging past the sharp shoulders of Dad's colleagues, the bruised shins of my soccer teammates, the gangly arms of his friends from residency. I imagine your pressed black dress crinkled when you sat down at a plastic table in the church gym, steadying yourself. The room smelled of basketballs and lemonade. People chattered in tight clusters, and a projector whirred through a photo slideshow. Dad at the beach. Dad with Mom. Dad at a game. Dad as a kid. Did you grab that plastic tabletop, hoping it could anchor you to the space, the time and place? Maybe you were still absorbing the service, thinking of the full church, the overflow room. The way light played through stained-glass stories. The way the wooden pews felt: hard, unyielding. At the reception, you said hi to Dad's sister and brother, but you didn't approach me. Maybe you slid by, recognizing, as you said, "Excuse me," that I had Dad's bone structure, his high cheeks, taut mouth. You had to have known it was me, his daughter. I read at the funeral, stood on my tiptoes the whole time I was at the lectern,

31

my clammy heels lifting out of new black flats. You flew to Columbia, South Carolina, from somewhere else to say goodbye to an old love, someone you hadn't spoken to in years. You paid for plane tickets and ate a lukewarm hotel breakfast before you got dressed in all black to sit in a church packed with people you didn't know to mourn an ex from decades ago, but you never introduced yourself to his family. Why? Was it too painful?

I think about you a lot, actually. Do you think about me? When I was seventeen, he died. When you were seventeen, you fell in love. You both grew up in Florida. You went to the same high school and started seeing each other when you were young. You dated for over half a decade, through college and a few years into Dad's med-school career. You must have wondered about his future, your future. Perhaps the two of you walked the warm shores of home, smooth sand clinging to your feet, sun pinking your faces, and maybe you thought, *I could do this forever*. Maybe at a Coen brothers film, the old theater seats sagging beneath you, you turned to look at Dad, his face lit up with excess blood, cheeks bathed in cinematic red, and you thought, *I love you*. You did, I know, love him. He loved you too.

I know you mostly through letters, the ones Dad mailed home while he went to school in the Northeast. I live in the Southwest now, about as far away as you can get from where he posted his postcards (without leaving the country, that is). It's a place where I can surgically remove myself from myself, my present from my past, and in fact, it's a prerequisite here. No one knows Dad, so when I walk to class or into coffee shops or down desert paths, I'm simply a woman, here. I'm not a woman whose dad died. There's so much distance between me. I'm only my full self at home. Maybe that's part of why I'm writing you, Hilda—I want to collapse the distance. I want to bring him closer to me.

Some afternoons, after I've swung open the door to my empty casita and shrugged off my teaching clothes, I'll sit in my reading chair warmed by the sun and think of those cold New England winters as I dig out one of Dad's old letters. After cracking open a sparkling water or an IPA, I'll start to read. The light-speed train of time and space shuttles me from my solitary home back to him, and back to you, too.

In the beginning, at Dartmouth, you were a frequent endnote. "Hilda told me that ya'll thought I might be better off flying home so I made reservations," he wrote in his precise, small handwriting. "Hilda told me you thought I was becoming a fancy dresser," he said, and "Hilda has a church function that night so I imagine she'll drop me off and be on her way." You weren't an afterthought but a steady undercurrent. Though you lived far apart, you must have talked often, your constant communication a given in his cramped letters and quick postcards. You were, for a few years, inextricably a part of each other's lives.

I wonder how that feels, that codependence. To be honest with you, I've worked hard to cut myself free from connection's net. I prickle when someone gets too close: everything is new and wrong. Whenever I begin to wonder what a man is doing while I'm writing in the library or walking up a cholla-studded trail or sipping chamomile in bed, I sigh. I make every beginning into an end. Every opening to commitment is a buttonhole sewn shut. Hilda, I'm scared of love because I lost it. You must know what that's like.

Is it weird for you that I write "Dad," not "Tom"? That his life continued and so did yours, separately? That he met a different woman, moved to a different state, married, went on vacations, had children, ate cheeseburgers and drank too much Diet Coke, and that you did the same, maybe, in a different state, hundreds of miles away, with different people, their faces too blurred for me to imagine? I wouldn't be surprised if it hurt you to think of me, if it reminded you that he lived, had a life, and died.

Do you want to know more about his life? We went whitewater rafting in Costa Rica, me, my brother, two cousins, and

Mom and Dad. Light fractured through greenery and glittered on the river. This was three years before his funeral. The most experienced guide at the center sat at the rear of our raft, steering our air-filled ship down dips and through foaming rapids with a confidence that comes only from time spent doing a thing over and over and over again. Still, we flipped. The river was cold. Underwater, Mom's knee gashed open on a rock. The cut was so deep it looked black with blood, and the skin that used to cover it hung limp around the wound. Later that night, on a scratchy hotel quilt, with scissors and sutures purchased from a local pharmacy, Dad sewed up her knee. It was remarkable the way he could put things back together, heal what seemed irredeemable.

When did you know it wouldn't last? Around '83, '84, you step out of the soupy background of his letters and become a subject. "I do like her a lot," he writes to his parents, "but have plenty of doubts yet so don't get worried. Tom has no intention of making any more commitments at this stage in his life."

On the back of a postcard captioned "The Window of Vulnerability," where a microwave flies into a living room (a weird postcard fitting of the weird man that bought it), he says, "I think my window of vulnerability is growing larger everyday . . . I love Hilda and at the same time she scares me—or rather our relationship scares me—It bothers her too."

On thick light blue paper, he prints, "Hilda and I have not broken up. We are in the process of redefining our relationship. . . . I don't think I'll (^ever) marry Hilda, but I'm not ready to rule the possibility out. She gives me a lot of comfort when I'm feeling down. She's my best friend (excluding family) and I'm not sure I'm ready to give up our relationship."

Later: "I really love her but I have trouble visualizing us together down the road. I know I could love her in my youth and old age but it's the years in between that scare me. I'm not sure we share enough to make it—I suspect we don't." Is it still painful, all these years later, to think of this, to remember the end?

Hilda, you broke up.

But in his letters, he never says he stopped loving you. Mom says you were head over heels for him. She says you would've married him if he'd asked. He loved you, but he couldn't see a future with you. How do you get over a break like that? Hilda, I'm asking: what happens when love isn't enough?

Sincerely,
Maddie

MOTHERS AND OTHER ORCAS

Everyone knows it: her grief is no longer new. Her name is Tahlequah, but most call her J-35. Though more truthfully, most don't know what to call her; they merely know her burden, the body she carries, in her mouth, on her nose, the child who died. Does she feel the cold water? Does she listen to the clicks and moans of family? She doesn't smell salt. Grief overwhelms. She only wants her baby to breathe.

For over two weeks, the mother carries her dead calf in mourning, nudging the open-mouthed corpse out of the water, waiting, wanting life's rift to heal. Her image plasters newspapers, and her body struggles on TV. Each morning, I check for news of her. My eyes still crusted with sleep, I search her name on my phone and let her face wake me up. I think of her throughout the day: eating a grilled cheese sandwich, taking the dog for a walk, escaping the heat indoors, I see her curved dorsal fin cut a black wake through water. For a while, her story is everywhere, and it sinks a hook in me; I let it reel me in.

When I feel the fishing line tug taut, I fly across the country to be closer to her grieving body. This sounds ridiculous, but I cannot shake the feeling that I need to be there. Behind my belly button, the ache of absence stretches. We're connected, me and this orca, and I feel her pull me close.

It's not odd that I find myself in killer whales; orcas are remarkably similar to humans. They have forty to fifty-six sharp teeth, five-digit bones within both pectoral flippers, a four-chambered heart, and a pair of lungs. Their brain-to-body ratio is second only to humans, and they have a gestation period of fifteen to eighteen weeks, which, while less than half of humans' typical forty weeks, is closer than that of many other mammals. Their attachments are similar too. Southern resident calves (so named because they live in the Salish Sea) travel directly beside their mothers and become emotionally attached, spending their entire lives swimming alongside them.

Twenty-eight years later, I wonder how my mom carries her miscarriage. After it happened, she and my dad flew from South Carolina to New Zealand to mourn, to get as far from themselves as possible. Their skin sighed as the air thinned, and when they fell asleep thirty-thousand feet above the ocean, I imagine their heads rolled together in communion. They were alone in this together. In New Zealand, my dad bungee-jumped off a bridge, and my mom looked at sheep. They wore white windbreakers and light-wash jeans. The land was green and rolling, and I imagine the air smelled crisp and biting, a grapefruit halved without sugar. Originally, they wanted three kids; my mom has two, and my dad is dead.

When my mom was born, a part of me was already within her—an egg in a fetus in a mother. I wonder, then, how I carry her loss, how I inherit her story, how grief nests us together. Two Matryoshka dolls, but am I within my mom or is she within me?

In a whale museum on San Juan Island, a small island off the coast of Seattle, I fit myself inside the ribs of a large orca skeleton. The bones are yellowed, smooth in places, rough in others. All the organs have been pulled out and the skin peeled away. Hung from the ceiling, what's left: the massive and empty blackfish skeleton. My head punctures the absence of life, and Mom snaps a picture of me trying to smile. We marvel that this whale skeleton, this singular carcass, can hold us both.

I read a printed plaque about who this whale once was. Moclips had a tall dorsal fin like a tissue plucked from the center, and nearer his body, a jagged nick, a quick blip in a heart monitor. He was a large whale, and his size kept him free. From the midsixties to the midseventies, orcas were netted and placed in captivity as tourist attractions (SeaWorld, Marineland, etc.), but Moclips was too large for easy transportation, his body too big to be boxed in a truck, his life too cumbersome to be contained, so each time he was captured, he was set free. His tall dorsal fin sliced open the water on reentry.

Still, Moclips saw his family taken, their bodies scooped up by black nets. Imagine how those losses weighed on him, how they broke him. Imagine the grief he carried. His body washed ashore on August 5, a day after my dad died.

My dad, for a long time, wanted to be a marine biologist. He grew up in Florida, never far from the ocean, so it's no surprise that it became a part of him. We went scuba diving together once, in warm waters, in the Bahamas, off Great Guana

Cay, him in front and me and my brother kicking along behind. The water was clear, and we watched our breath ascend all the way to the surface, where it broke its bubble form. Light draped over everything, the bright sand, the shimmering fish, our bodies. Mom was there too, but she swam behind us, outside our vision, making sure we didn't scrape against fire coral or swim too close to the moray lurking in crevices. I didn't see her, though of course she was there. Looking back, I wonder how she felt, trying to protect us from something as massive as the ocean. Helpless, I imagine.

A school of silver fish tornadoed to the left, a red and green reef stood sentry on the right, and in front of me, in the cracked open ocean floor, a blacktip shark lumbered through the fissure. Its tail swept up sand, its journey slow and easy. Mom, my brother, and I hovered over the shifting ocean floor and watched Dad follow the shark, its body as big as his, both of them flippering, sliding away from us, through the clear ocean water.

The greatest threat to whales is humans. This isn't because we're hunting them or intentionally harming them; it's because we don't pay attention to them, meaning we don't consider how our actions affect them. Or worse, we just don't care. Orcas have finely tuned echolocation, and their clicking sonar can separate one salmon species from another, but boats drown the mammals in noise, disrupt their echolocation, their ability to see, and blind them to distance, to sustenance and danger. We harvest salmon and deprive them of food. We leached PCBs as we leach PBDEs. These flame-retardant chemicals are carcinogenic, and though no longer manufactured in the United States, they remain in materials still in use from when they were mass-produced. The chemicals eke from paints, plastics, and well-oiled motors, magnifying up the food chain, gathering in orca fat like a child's mouth gathering teeth. These toxins hamper the immune system, the nervous system, and the reproductive system.

Lulu, an orca who washed ashore in 2016, was never able to conceive, likely because of PCBs. Her white belly was hugged by black, and her body sagged on the wet, dark rocks of a cold shoreline. From her lip down to her flipper, blood rusted her body. She is the most contaminated marine mammal found to date, with her blubber containing more than one hundred times the level of safe toxicity. In response to the shock of finding the poisoned female, one scientific advisor said, "Lulu was fairly old, so she will have accumulated [PCBs] over her lifetime and that's the reason she had such high levels. It's a legacy she'd carried from her early years."

There's a long list of toxic mothers in literature: Gertrude from *Hamlet*, Charlotte from *Lolita*, Mrs. Bennett from *Pride and Prejudice*, Medea from Greek mythology. Watch a Disney movie, *The Jungle Book*, *The Little Mermaid*, *The Fox and The Hound*. Watch *Aladdin*, *Tarzan*, *Beauty and the Beast*. Watch *Bambi*. The mothers are absent or dead. Without them, their children can go on journeys of growth and adventure. The mothers birth the children, and their job is done. The child's story starts at birth, after separation from the mother. This all means that mothers don't get stories of their own, but I want my mom to have her own story; I want to give her a piece of mine.

I think of how different I would be if my mom weren't here, if I had grown up without her. She taught me what it means to care. This week, she called me, upset that she had had the dog spayed. "How silly," she said, "but I'm taking motherhood away from her." She comes home from work, sits down on an empty couch, and closes her eyes while the dog flops beside her, then places her paw on her breastbone, pining to be seen. My mom is annoyed by this, the fact that she has no down time, the fact that she comes home from work and cannot close her eyes without another needy body needling her, but mostly, truthfully, she loves this. She comes home from work to a dog who loves her, not just an empty house. She's a child psychologist, and she sits on the floor with kids every weekday, watching them build with Legos, helping them imagine worlds larger than their homes, impossible worlds, worlds where love exists without loss.

Mom says I was a happy child, though I don't always remember it this way. I had severe separation anxiety and hated leaving her arms. We had an elaborate goodbye ritual to ease me into her absence, but, of course, it was a way to ease her into my absence too—she didn't want to leave me either. Mom would say, "See you later, alligator," and I'd reply, "In a while, crocodile." "In a shake, garden snake." "In a blue moon, you big baboon." We kept going until we ran out of animals and out of time. In a grainy video of my kindergarten class, a net of children sits on the ground, crisscross applesauce. The video pans from a teacher in the front playing guitar to children singing along. Everyone claps to "If you're happy and you know it clap your hands." The camera swims, passing over glue-crusted fingers and pulled-at pigtails, and in the corner, there's a small redheaded child, me, sitting in the assistant teacher's lap, crying. I missed my mom.

When calves become separated from their families, they yearn for connection. In the early 2000s, Luna surfaced hundreds of miles from his family, in Nootka Sound, the rocky green coast off Vancouver. He was lonely, rolling in the deep blue water, slapping the surface to spray no one. His dorsal fin cut through the water cleanly, and the white patch behind his eye glittered just below the surface. He swam to boats, nudged their hulls, and pushed their bows, reaching out for physical touch, for presence in the wake of absence. He looked for family and found love in things that wound. There were reunification efforts, but Luna never returned to his pod. He swam to a tugboat and was pulled into the motor's blades. His mother, faraway, died two years later. To paraphrase E. M. Forester, the prince died, and then the queen died of grief.

There's this, too: three days before Luna arrived in Vancouver, the traditional territory of the Mowachaht/Muchalaht Nation, the tribe was in mourning. Ambrose Maquinna, their elder chief, one in an ancient line of patriarchs, had died. But, before he did, he promised to come back as a killer whale. Days later, Luna swam in their sea.

When we land in Seattle, on our way to see the whales, both of us looking through the plane's muddled windows, onto the tarmac, and into the dark night, past shadowed firs and under cumulus clouds, through fire haze and into the past, my mom whispers, "I can't believe it's been six years." Even now, I wake up from dreams in which both my parents are alive, and in the early morning mist, I have to puzzle out which one of them died. Before they married, my dad calculated, based on average life expectancy, that he and my mom would die less than a year apart. He was scared to be alone.

On the boat, land disappears into distance. A sailboat leans into thick mud at low tide, caught until the water returns. My face is pink from the sun and the wind and the cold. Mom keeps her hand on my shoulder, and in front of us, the ocean winks. "I hope we see an orca, for your sake," she says. On the way to the water, I wouldn't stop talking about the black-and-white whales, how playful they are, how social, how delicate. Ahead of the boat, beneath the blue day: a puff of mist. The captain calls all fifteen passengers to the bow, and the humpback's tail slides out of the water before gliding back in. The emergence is not unlike being born, not unlike giving birth, sudden and shocking, even when expected. Six minutes pass before we see another spray of air. This time, the humpback heaves its body above the surface, its eye turns skyward, its body glints, and its tail flickers. "I think that was an orca," Mom says, grabbing my arm, but it's only the humpback moving closer. We stay on the water for hours, and still, we never see an orca. I tell Mom I'm happy seeing the humpback, watching its body disappear and reappear, and I *am* happy. There is no denying the beauty of the marine creature, its heft and fragile movements coalescing without reason. The nature guide explains that it's rare to see the solitary humpback migrating, more common, here, to find families of orcas, and yet, I wonder how to explain that I want what's common, that I'd take the moving bodies of orcas co-mingling over a breaching humpback any day. As the boat speeds back to shore, I keep looking into the distance.

It's important to know this: whale watching is an ethically complicated business. Boats, even at a safe distance, rupture orcas' daily lives, affecting their resting, their foraging, and feeding. The presence of an outsider can create stress and alter the shape of a day. One or two boats occasionally isn't harmful, but the repetition of boat after boat hour after hour adds up. It's the pattern that pains them. "Females can even stop pro-ducing enough milk for their calves, which can decrease the survival rate of their young," says Dr. David Lusseau, a marine biologist. "Ultimately the viability of a pod can be threatened." The constant intrusion of boats can kill the orcas. But whale watching could save the mammals, too. The more people see these creatures, the more likely they are to fall in love with their sleek skin, their playful breaches, their familial bonds. The more people love these creatures, the more they want to save them, and isn't it always love that saves us? Isn't it?

My mom's father left her family when she was young. Her mother once placed her in the front seat of a car and drove across town. My mom did her math homework as they rode under a grey sky, past half-built skyscrapers, under interstate bridges, and over small flowing creeks. I imagine Mom hunched over her lined notebook, pressing the pencil point firmly into the paper, ovaling her zeros and sharply angling all her isosceles as my grandmother pointed to a trailer, and, inside it, my grandfather and the woman he was having an affair with.

My mom's parents divorced when she was in middle school, and her relationship with her father began to unspool. "You could be a good dental hygienist," he told her; she earned her doctorate in clinical psychology. He found it impossible to see her as who she was, and distance spun out from this principal misunderstanding. Eventually, their relationship ran out of thread. Her father wasn't invited to her wedding. This year would have been my parents' twenty-six-year anniversary. When my dad was dying, he told my mom, "I'm sorry. I'm leaving you, just like your dad." He wasn't scared of being alone anymore; he was scared of hurting her.

Orcas learn language from their mothers. Each pod, or extended family, has its own dialect, its own collection of whines and cries, whistles and clicks, that net meaning. The mother shows the child a salmon and repeats the word. Salmon, salmon, salmon. She noses toward the fish. Salmon, salmon,

salmon. The child looks past the haze of water and under the choppy surface, through the rumple of sea life, and into the slippery being sliding its way through the ocean. Salmon, salmon, salmon. It's through repetition that orcas learn to speak, through maternal guidance that they learn to listen.

I ask my mom if she often thinks of her miscarriage. It happened two years before my brother was born, three years before I was born. "No," she says, before pausing, then continuing, "It was hard, but it would've been harder if I hadn't had you and your brother." I know she means this, that her love for us is unadulterated, but I also know that some losses can't be filled. I imagine the blood, streaming down a toilet bowl, inking into clear water, washing away, leaving a pink stain under the porcelain rim.

In 1974, only seventy-one Southern Resident orcas were counted, and while that number grew to ninety-eight in 1995, following the Marine Mammal Protection Act (which required special permits for live capture), the family has been slowly collapsing since. Think of the noise pollution. Think of the salmon, overfished. Think of the chemicals, the toxins. In 2001, eighty orcas were counted. In 2016, seventy-eight. In 2019, seventy-three. Killer whales are now listed as endangered under the Endangered Species Act, meaning they are at risk of becoming extinct, of dying out, disappearing completely.

The summer I start looking for whales is the summer I tell my mom I'm not sure I want children. As I say the words, I remember, several years ago, a child fell at my feet on the tiled floor of a pizza restaurant. It must have felt cold to him, though it was summer and warm crust steamed the air. He looked up at me with eyes the color of light cracks in water. His yellow shirt was bunched on one arm, and I bent down to pick him up, arms outstretched. I bent to pick him up, but when I hinged back up, my arms were still outstretched, empty: I hadn't touched the child. I couldn't pick him up; I didn't know how to right a fall. Picking him up wouldn't revert the tumble, couldn't undo the injury, so I stood there, in the middle of a crowded pizza restaurant, with empty hands holding the absence of a child. He began to cry, still on the floor, and one of his mothers hurried to pick him up. She placed him against her warm skin and pressed his head against her caged heart, and I stood there, alone and ashamed.

Orcas, being mammalian, absorb nutrients through their mothers' milk. It's one of the many ways mothers provide comfort to their offspring. The children swim beside their mothers, and the mothers suckle them. Initially, their milk is extremely high in fat, but the percentage decreases over time. It's essential for calves to synthesize blubber so that they can protect themselves from the cold and survive the winter waters (hence the high fat content). The mother, in this way, provides the calf with the raw material for insulation. She helps her babies stay warm.

The problem with this circles back to PCBs and PBDEs. These toxins build up in the mothers' milk through bioaccumulation. The toxicity levels become too high for the mother, so when the children nurse, the mothers unknowingly, unconsciously, perhaps unwillingly, offload toxins in their milk. The mothers survive by sharing death with their daughters. The daughters need their mothers, and the mothers need their daughters, and what they share is hurt.

When cells flow out of one individual and into another, it's called microchimerism ("micro" as in small, "chimera" as in a monster with mismatched parts, *or* "chimera" as in impossible hope). Normally, an organism won't share its cells, nor will it accept the cells of others; we prefer to stay hermetically sealed. It can be risky, sharing too much of yourself, letting others in.

Of course, there are exceptions. The most common form of microchimerism is a mother harboring cells from her children or a miscarriage. During pregnancy, cells can be passed through the placenta, from fetus to mother. So Mom holds me, holds my brother, holds her broken fetus. Less commonly, though still possible, fetuses can harbor cells from the mother. Mom contains me, and I contain Mom.

Now my mom adds the phrase "if you want children" to the ends of sentences when she talks about my future. She loves children, loves the way they teeter toward pools without fear of falling in, the way they reach toward her so openly in want. She wants grandchildren because she truly loves mothering, because she loves being surrounded by humans who love her and whom she can love. She says "if you want children," and I can hear the sadness in her voice. I wonder if she wants another piece of my dad in the world, too, if she wants to see his Roman nose again, feel his thick hair, hear his laugh, listen to his guffaw one more time.

I remember eating at a seafood restaurant years ago, me, Mom, Dad, and my brother. Mom and Dad had just come back from Boston, where Dad's primary oncologist worked. During the day, when they weren't shut up in the hospital, they explored the city, trying to distract themselves. This time, they went to the aquarium, where they marveled at archerfish.

These fish shoot their prey down with a stream of water that arches over the water's surface, an attack as surprising as it is effective. At dinner, while listening to this story, I was staring at the tank lit up behind Mom, watching the small fish bob along, thinking of the pursed mouths of fish whistling water into air, when I felt a stream of cold water hit my face. "It was the archerfish!" Mom said, glass of water still in hand. She'd spit the stream at me. It's the only time I've laughed so hard I cried.

Years later, Mom tells me on that trip to Hopkins, Dad told her that if he died, she had to be the fun grandparent. She says that in that moment, at the restaurant, sitting down to fresh cornbread and hot hushpuppies, she was trying to show him she could do it.

Tahlequah carrying her child to grieve is not unusual. In fact, many animals touch their dead children while they can, warm their cold bodies, imprint the contours of their child into memory. The mothers want to remember their hard bones, their soft stomachs, the life they could have had. "What is unusual," says Ken Balcomb, founder of the Center for Whale Research, "is the length of time she is carrying [her child] and the critical photo-documentation we are able to do over this time of grieving."

Grief doesn't end, but at some point, people outside the loss stop looking. Only those within it remain vigilant to absence.

These days, Mom is considering moving back up the East Coast to be with her mother. My grandmother has started forgetting things, repeating herself. On phone calls, she asks three times where I want to settle down and twice she tells me about the dog she got months ago, a pit bull named Gracie. "Gracie!" she yells, then returns to the call as though we'd just started our conversation. In short: my grandmother is losing her mind. When I call my grandmother while I'm home in South Carolina, I always get off the phone by asking if she wants to talk to my mom. I sit down on the couch and listen to my mom pace the floor, answering the same questions minutes apart, her voice always patient and steady, a mother's voice.

People say I take after my dad, and it's true that we have the same angled jaw, the same nose-to-the-grindstone work ethic, the same way of stifling laughs at our own jokes, smile spreading into wide open mouth, but it's true, too, that within me there is also, always, my mom. My mom and I have the same eyes, brown in the center reaching for green. We have small wrists that fit child-size watches. We can unhinge our jaws, fit our fists in our mouths, swallow more than others think. We have the same hole in our lives, and we know its blood better than anyone else.

At home, Mom looks at me from under the blue comforter. "Oh God, this is disgusting," she says. I ask if she wants some water before she takes another sip of the cloudy liquid in her hand. She nods as her lips pucker. I remember how she cared for me when I was sick, and my body mimics how she held me, how she cooked me soup and rubbed my back. The prep is the worst part of the colonoscopy: for twenty-four hours, Mom can only have liquids. She runs to the bathroom as the foul-tasting medicine cleans out her colon. She drinks water only to have it come right back out. When I visit her, I usually sleep on the right side of the bed—it used to be her side before Dad died, but she moved over to his indent on the left after. Tonight, though, she reclaims the right side, the one closer to the bathroom, and I sleep in Dad's old spot.

Almost a decade earlier, he'd done this routine with her, brought her fluids and rubbed her back. In the morning, I drive her to the hospital and drink weak coffee from a Styrofoam cup in the waiting room. After the procedure, I sit by her bedside while she sleeps. A closed curtain separates us from the rest of the patients, but my chair is stiff and an awkward distance from the bed, so while I can't reach her from where I sit, I watch her. She looks so small in the bed, her back turned toward me, her breathing deep, a sleeping newborn. The nurse pats her back and calls her name to wake her up. Mom's eyes are saucers, and she slurs her words; it's like gauze has been stuffed in her mouth. She seems so defenseless—I almost cry. Like last time, when Dad brought her, the doctor finds polyps, which, by definition, are precancerous. He shows me pictures of the slimy growths inside her as he explains that he cut them out and sent them to the lab. "My husband was a doctor," Mom says, "Tom Norris." The doctor remembers him: "I knew him well." He doesn't know what else to say, so he hands me the sheet that captures Mom's toxic insides.

I sometimes imagine dying, letting the steering wheel swivel toward the tree, stepping into the crosswalk and feeling or not feeling my body be crushed. How many bodies must Mom identify, claim as her own? More often, I imagine the opposite. One morning, maybe, or perhaps late afternoon, my mom will step outside onto slick ice, surprising ice, and she will fall, crack her head, bone rearranging itself into a gruesome mosaic, red slipping over the cold ground, gray matter oozing. Her dog will huddle beside her, but my dad won't be there to call an ambulance, to cradle her blooming skull. I won't be there either.

This is what scares us: solitary loneliness. We can sit together in Dad's death, call each other when we hear the Sex Pistols or eat a Honeybell orange, and we don't have to explain why because our stories are the same. We can be lonely together, the two of us as one, but what happens when there's no one to be lonely with?

Tahlequah carries her dead child over one thousand miles. Her dives are stilted and deep, her breathing ragged. For seventeen days, she keeps the cold body of her child on her nose, in her mouth. The body, sometimes, begins to sink, slipping off her nose, falling through the water, but each time, Tahlequah dives down, nudges the child to the surface, takes a breath, and keeps moving with her baby. Every morning, Mom and I click on the TV to see if she is still carrying the child. The day we land in Seattle, Tahlequah drops the corpse. The orange six-foot-long body sinks, deteriorating on the ocean floor. The carcass bloats. The skin is nibbled off by scavengers, the muscle tugged away. On the ocean floor, I imagine the cleaned bones settled into the dark muck of the seabed housing microscopic bacteria, the gutted rib cage still big enough to hold the both of us.

STILL HEARTS

irst: fixation. Formaldehyde is forced into former bloodstreams, killing bacteria and stalling decomposition. Then skin and fat are peeled from the body, shucked from organs and innards. The body is disassembled into separate display pieces. The heart is pulled from its home and soaked in acetone, where water and water-solvent fats dissolve. When the hull-organ is full of the simplest and smallest ketone, it's moved for what is officially called forced impregnation. The acetone is boiled away in a vat of polyester or epoxy resin or silicone rubber. The chosen polymer now plumps the heart. The organ is clamped, strung, pinned, and stuck. The body is cured with gas or heat or light. Inside a glass box, the waxy red organ sits still, on display for children and parents who paid twenty dollars to enter a Body Worlds exhibit and look at a human being made lifeless. Anatomically, the heart is accurate, but the veins and chambers and blocked-up arteries don't strike me as real, and I imagine this is because the heart is unmoving and silent.

Gray's Anatomy, a textbook I find in a box of my dad's old things, notes that it's the heart's "rhythmic contraction" that curls blood through the body, and when I consider the heart, I consider sound. I listen to *Palais de Mari* played by Sabine Liebner. The piano notes vibrate in the air, hanging alone. Before my body records the singularity of the previous key, before it can catalogue and archive the feeling of sound, a new note is played, disrupting my music memory. Two keys that should sound discordant stretch into silence. My chest tightens, and I wonder if this is what it feels like to be known. The notes continue, out of sync. Their pattern shuffles, shapeshifting into a new form. The notes tangle together like hair on a windy day, knotting and unknotting. My body responds differently and unpredictably each time, and by the silent end, I've looped myself around myself, and I'm unsure how to straighten.

Hypertrophic cardiomyopathy is a condition where the heartwalls are too thick and the heartmuscle too big. I was checked for the genetic condition in seventh grade, when my face was oily but not yet pitted in pimples. My dad's dad had died from it. His heart stopped in his sleep and stayed stopped. My grandmother woke one morning, rolled over, and found a cold body where her husband had been. My parents took me to a heart specialist, and in a cold room, a nurse asked me to undress. I didn't know whether I should take off my training bra, so I kept it on, wanting to hide myself as much as possible. When the nurse returned, she asked me to remove my "tank top." I lay naked under a thin paper sheet that crunched when I moved. The doctor put cold jelly over my heart and nuzzled an ultrasound stick into my skin. My heart was not too big, but a monitor showed how quickly it was beating. I tried not to squirm.

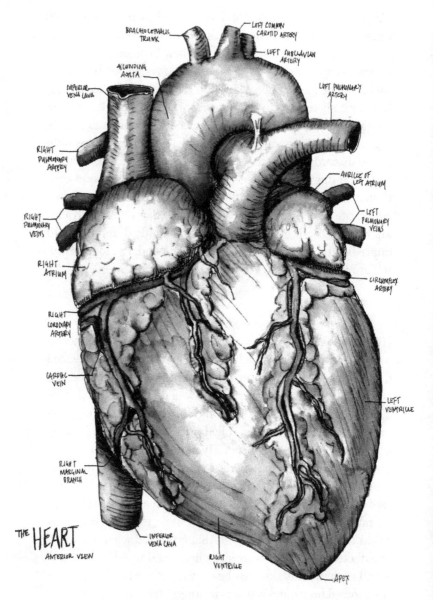

THE HEART
ANTERIOR VIEW

BRACHIOCEPHALIC TRUNK

LEFT COMMON CARTID ARTERY

LEFT SUBCLAVIAN ARTERY

ASCENDING AORTA

SUPERIOR VENA CAVA

LEFT PULMONARY ARTERY

RIGHT PULMONARY ARTERY

RIGHT PULMONARY VEINS

AURICLE OF LEFT ATRIUM

LEFT PULMONARY VEINS

RIGHT ATRIUM

CIRCUMFLEX ARTERY

RIGHT CORONARY ARTERY

CARDIAC VEIN

LEFT VENTRICLE

RIGHT MARGINAL BRANCH

INFERIOR VENA CAVA

RIGHT VENTRICLE

APEX

Figure 1. What is a heart worth when it's stopped?

Annie Dillard said to put death up front, so here it is: my dad died when I was seventeen. He was a doctor and was diagnosed with cancer. Less than a year after they found a mass in his pancreas, he went to the hospital for a blockage in his digestive tract. He'd been carrying around a plastic yellow tub, throwing up water and bile as he turned away from conversations. One day, in a hot tub, I was reading him an essay, one I'd written about him. I got my love of words from Dad, though he was dyslexic, so he lingered on each syllable, savoring the sound. I tried to read slowly for him. I looked up as he retched; his back twisted toward me, the knobs of his spine curling through skin. When he turned to face me, he said, "Maybe another day." In the hospital, the doctors told my mom it was not a blockage but more cancer. At home, my mom told me it was not a blockage but the end. We went back to the hospital that night, and I finished reading him my essay. Family friends dropped off fried chicken and sugar cookies. "Eat," they said. I pinched off a streak of greasy, crispy skin. I pinched off a bit of crumbled cookie. They didn't taste like anything. At night, my dad pulled his head from his pillow with effort. I could hear his muscles straining. I leaned down and he kissed my forehead for the last time. His lips were dry, and skeins of dead skin wove through them. I pulled away and his lips were still pursed, his eyes still closed, and it took his body more than a beat to recognize I was gone. I threw up on the side of the car as Mom drove me home in the dark. The next morning, Dad's heartbeat stopped.

The heart is a verb, physically. Its interior is gummed with papillary muscle. Sunk to the bottom of the organ are two ventricles, the pumping pistons of the body, thick walled and strong. The atria, nestled above, gather blood back from the body, from the veins that bring the tide in. Old blood enters the right atrium and is forced into the right ventricle. The blood then moves toward the lungs, propelled by ventricle strength, where it sheds carbon dioxide and redresses in oxygen. The stream continues, crisscrossing to the left atrium, where it's forced into the left ventricle, shuttled out of the aorta and into arteries and smaller capillaries, where nutrients are deposited. The tired blood drains into venules and veins and busses back to the right atrium, where it will begin again. Everything is always in motion, and the heart is a verb, symbolically too. It races, skips, leaps, and flutters. I ♥ you means I love you means the heart means to love.

My dad was the one that took me to Body Worlds. He wanted to show me what he saw inside all of his patients, inside himself, inside me. We walked through the white-walled exhibit with dozens of other families, and he kept one hand on my shoulder, the other free to point out different pieces of the body: a system of nerves, a chest cavity cut concave, a heart flayed open. I imagined these innards were what he saw when he heard a cough, a wheeze, a stuttered breath. At an early age, I learned to look at bodies through the lens of my dad.

Palais de Mari translates to "Husband's Palace," which is a truth I didn't consider when naming it my heartsong. I don't know that I'll ever marry. I enjoy weddings and look forward to friends' weddings, envision their twinkle lights under giant redwoods and the tall arced ceilings of old Southern churches, but I don't imagine I'll have a wedding of my own. Or, rather, when I try to imagine my wedding, I see my dress with lace sleeves slipping over my wrists, and I see my mom with her hair hairsprayed and her feet in small heels and she is crying as we walk down the aisle and I see my family and friends but I never see a betrothed. I have never said "I love you" to a romantic partner principally because I have never loved them.

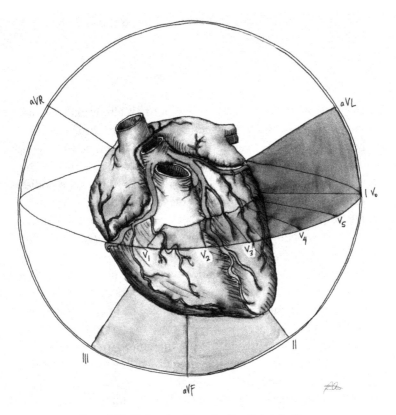

Figure 2. What is the value of love when it can't circle back?

Clear and clean lungs sit next to a smoker's blackened and tarred pair. Body Worlds aims to promote preventative health-care. Dr. Whalley and Dr. von Hagens, the married brains be-hind the endeavor, hope their plastinated bodies and organs expose the beauty and fragility of human anatomy. The thin mesh of capillaries curl around the open air, a cracked wind-shield. The doctors want visitors to explore practical questions about the body: How many gallons of blood does the heart pump each day? How can these gallons disappear? How can their absence be present?

In still-sweaty sheets, I fit my head into his elbow and put two fingers to his neck. He'd already had me palm his broken collarbone, an injury that went unnoticed for so long it never healed, and I'd let him bite my shoulder, a peach dribbling juice. The morning light fell on us in slats as we explored how two bodies could see each other. We were both writers, though words felt less important when we were together. It was about the movement of our bodies. We did things like: hike and drink red wine by water we found in the desert. He struggled opening the dark bottle, broke the corkscrew, and pulled at the plug with his dirt-lined fingernails. I sat against the cold rocks and watched his arms strain against the seal. Eventually, he opened it, and we drank. When the sun began to drop, we started hiking back, and though we lost the trail more than once, we made it to the car in time to drive down the mountain as the sun set. Later, in bed, when we were outlining each other's bodies, he said, "My pulse is over here" and placed my fingers an inch up and over. For a moment, we didn't move. His freckled arm stretched out behind my back, his ulna to my temporal, my ulna to his sternum, his femur to my patella, my phalanges against his carotid, his eyes trying to meet mine. "Yep," I said, "still alive."

I play *Palais de Mari* on repeat. I listen to it on my phone, but I imagine the thin disc of a record, its heft and fragility, its ruts that make music. I think about what it would feel like to flip the cool vinyl in my hand, then place it on a turntable, let the needle settle into its tracks. The song is almost thirty minutes long, and I listen in cars and on planes and walking to work.

I listen in transit. I see a tree nodding in the breeze, clouds clotting over metal wings, two dogs connected by a leash. I smell old French fries and newborn babies and the smoky drip of mesquite trees. The air is hot and thin while it is wet and soupy. I listen to the song, and time accordions itself. When I hear the notes spiral staircase into composition, a new layer of space is added over the same film. It's a different scene but underneath, the same soundtrack.

The heart, these days, is a sentimental sore spot, though it wasn't always. The ancient Egyptians speculated it housed the soul and was home to intellect, while Aristotle assumed it wombed reason. Galen suspected it birthed emotions, though not love, which was displaced to the slimy liver. It wasn't until medieval Europe, when Christianity threw together Celt and Viking imagery with courtly love standards, that the heart was pinned with love. Now, it's fickle; it's blind; it's unreasonable. To write about it is sentimental, self-absorbed, navel gazing. The heart's story is overplayed, overwrought, trite. Consider, though, that initially the heart was thought to be smart and sensitive, that emotional intelligence was once detected and honored within the pulpy organ. The heart might be denigrated, but it carries a noble history.

Hypertrophic cardiomyopathy is a common cause for cardiac arrest in otherwise seemingly healthy people. You are running and then you are not. You are speaking and then you can't. You are alive, in this world, where the desert dirt smells like hope after rain and where the streets don't have streetlamps so the stars poke through and where he walks you home and protects you from cacti spines and where he kisses you and then he doesn't. The heartcells are too big and the blood can't push through. The organ no longer pulses. The circulatory rivers stagnate. The body stops. You die.

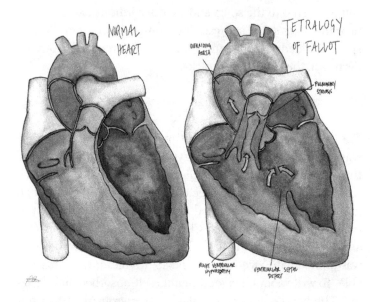

Figure 3. Why am I always returning to the break?

My dad's stethoscope is a sticky black Y with an elaborate curled L on the coin that he pressed against hundreds of backs and breasts to listen to hearts. "Littmann Quality" is printed around the L, and black tubing traces the neck of the Y to its ears, where silver emerges and then cuts back to black. He used to sling the stethoscope around his neck, curl it over his collar, let it jump against his chest as he walked. He'd come home from work with a clipped stack of three-by-five cards stuck in his button-down's pocket and the stethoscope draped around his neck. After taking off his jacket and grabbing a snack, he'd sit at the kitchen table and get to work. I used to sit across from him. Now, his stethoscope hangs on the hook where he used to hang his coat. The earpieces are like olives stuck onto silver tubes, and I pull them opposite each other and place them in my ears. The world muffles. I tap the L and hear a soft kick drum. I push the L under my shirt and over my heart. My engine churns in another world.

In the center of my dad's *Color Atlas of Human Anatomy* is a section on the thorax with over ten pages of colored heart images. The first pages capture the gray-brown muscle in context, nestled in crinkled and fanned gray-brown bodies. Then, the heart is removed, cut away from the self, pictured alone, a red ribbon of major cardiac vessels encircling it. Then, the heart is sliced open, its popped bubblegum insides exposed. Then, casts of cardiac vessels, blue and red threads dancing into thick lace, veins tangling into bramble, red over blue over red over blue, the two enmeshed so completely that I can't see through to the other side.

Morton Feldman, the composer of *Palais de Mari*, hovered between categories, one foot in narrative richness and the other in the pure pleasure of sound. In interviews, his black hair is slicked back and curves in at his chin like a child's overwrought drawing. He wears thick glasses that magnify his eyes, and he is either open-mouthed laughing with his lower lip slipping out to make room for noise, or he is still, mouth shut. In a way, his breaks and contradictions in character come through in his art, too. His music is rational and irrational, linear and circular, one thing while maintaining the possibility of its opposite. Instead of the traditional musical notes along a staff, he wrote several pieces using "graphic notation." For example, in one piece, open boxes sit next to each other on a page, and musicians choose a note within the range to play. In another, musicians choose the length of a pitch. Of his music, Feldman wrote in "The Anxiety of Art," "Faced with a mystery about divinity, according to the riddle, we must always hover, uncertain, between the two possible answers."

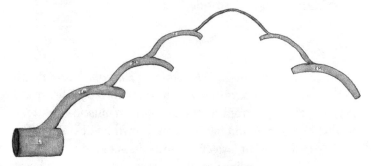

Figure 4. Is there movement in indecision?

After a record swap, I walked downtown with friends. The four of us shuffled along the dark streets in shifting pairs. The night was the kind of blue that makes construction sites with scaffolds and flapping tarps look romantic. The restaurant glowed warmly as we approached, the inverse of a bruise on otherwise unblemished skin. Its front was wide, clean windows punctuated by rustic wood. In the corner, we ordered cocktails and dipped tortilla chips in salsa. I imagined we looked like an Edward Hopper painting. I mentioned I'd been to this restaurant once before, on a date, where we left to sit close to each other and listen to soft music. Across the table, his pupils dilated, and he told me I was beautiful. "Why did you break it off?" a friend asked. I didn't know how to answer. Later, someone suggested you can get over anything if you try.

Human bodies have been preserved for centuries, naturally and artificially. Cold and dry heat keep remains intact, as do freezing and certain soils. Bodies sunk in peat bogs, whether purposefully or by happenstance, retain their wrinkles from 8,000 BCE. Ancient Egyptians mummified humans, pulling out all their organs except for the heart, which would speak for itself in the afterlife, and Peru, too, was known for its mummies, which were dried for conservation. Alexander the Great was kept in honey, and Xin Zhui, the Lady of Dai of the Western Han dynasty, was preserved remarkably well, her cheeks still apple round. During the Renaissance, Europeans injected liquids such as water, ink, and wax into the body to allow for medical study. Toward the end of the 1800s, formaldehyde began becoming the norm, and Body Worlds' preferred plastination was developed in the 1920s. The preservation of humans is not new, but Body Worlds has attracted more than forty million visitors since 1995. It's the precipice that attracts people, that attracts me. There is a precarity in the posed models as they teeter between life and death.

Memories of my dad are slipping away. Did he teach me about the heart? Did he trace vein and artery canals with me? We used to swim in the ocean, brace our bodies against the waves or dive under them. The cool slap of water shocked our stomachs, spitting drips onto our shoulders. We'd laugh and taste salt. Underneath the surface, the sea tickled every hair on our bodies, reminding us of our edges. On land, we drove around in his silver SUV, and he sang in a rough, low voice, steel wool circling a pan. At home, I sat on the kitchen counter, a shallow cut bleeding from my leg, red beading against grated skin. His hands were calloused and soft and he placed the band-aid deliberately, smoothing it over my skin before pulling away.

Hypertrophic cardiomyopathy is a genetic condition. Just one mutant copy of the MYH7 gene or the MYBPC3 gene or the TNNT2 or TNNI3 leads to abnormal heart composition. These genes create proteins for sarcomeres, the thick and thin filaments controlling cardiac contraction. The different filaments kiss and then break apart. The sarcomeres' pattern of love creates the heart's pulse. Two actions are necessary for regular cardiac functioning: the thick and thin must come together. The thick and thin must break apart.

I pulled his face to mine outside a wine bar with stained glass windows. He licked his lips a lot, and they were both soft and dry. When we kissed, I thought of nothing else. For a moment, we were stuck in honey. The traffic lights hummed red, the brick pressed against my back, he pressed against my ribs. My fingers dug for his carotid, as though searching for life, as though wanting death. At some point, we stopped kissing. I didn't love him because I couldn't. He didn't love me because he didn't. Still: we used our hearts to stay alive.

PHANTOM LONGING

t a bar, a man sits down across from me. I watched him order his drink, and he looked at me, and I looked back. He takes this as an invitation to sit across from me; he isn't wrong. I'm feeling reckless, empty. We make small talk, and I let myself think about his neck. As he speaks, tendons press against his skin, making their shape known before disappearing from sight. They are thick and strong, turgid stalks, and then they are gone. I imagine sliding my hand over the slope of his neck, from the curve below his chin down to his collarbone, the smoothness of it. Would he jump at my touch? Would his vocal cords tense? His shirt is loose at the neck, and there is a gap between its collar and the base of his neck. I wonder what his sweat tastes like.

Desire is like this: hunger scraping the back of my throat like a car bottoming out, careening down my spine, crashing, spectacularly, below. Rubberneck just to see it, the flush, the want. I mean "want" in both senses, desire and lack. There's an emptiness that only desire can hollow out. Through yearning, I feel the edges of myself. Longing is the shape of absence.

In *A Lover's Discourse*, Roland Barthes writes, "But isn't desire always the same, whether the object is present or absent? Isn't the object *always* absent?" He means you can't long for what you have; there must be distance, a chasm, between you and the object of your want.

I hit the height of puberty when Dad fell ill. I pushed tampons to the bottom of my backpack while Dad had a port surgically implanted above his heart. I nicked the crooks of my knees when shaving while doctors counted the dwindling white blood cells in his body. As my body grew into a sexual being, Dad's body attacked itself. When my hips widened, when my breasts filled, he was dead. I learned to want in grief, and I'm not sure how to separate the two. I'm not sure I want to.

At times, desire can feel like death. In *A Lover's Discourse*, Barthes recounts a Buddhist koan in which a master holds a disciple's head underwater until he has no more air in his lungs. The water burns his throat, and his eyes go dark. The master holds the disciple underwater until he touches the edge of death, and then he pulls him back. The master says, "When you have craved truth as you crave air, then you will know what truth is." For Barthes, the absence of the desired is the master. It's the absence, then, that holds our head underwater. It's this absence, then, this lack, that teaches us what longing is.

He keeps one hand on the bicycle seat, the other wrapped around the handlebars. His arms strain taut, stiff. They're shadowed in the alley because there are no streetlights here, very few in the whole city, actually. This is by design—the city doesn't want to pollute the sky with light; they leave it empty for a reason. The only light comes from the sky, and tonight, there are no clouds, so the stars speckle the dark like a swath of freckles.

He's walked me home from the brewery where we accidentally sat too close to the band. We couldn't talk over the music, though we tried, yelling in each other's ears, breath sticky with wheat, but it was no use; the speakers shook over everything. Eventually we sat, listened to the bluegrass band, and said nothing. In the dark alley, outside my casita, we've run out of things to say, and the IPA tastes bright in my mouth, and the air smells like dirt, and a melon baller has scooped all the air out of my lungs, and the gravel crunches as he leans forward, and we kiss.

The men I long for are mostly projections built around a few true features. Sarcasm, a strong jaw, a deep, easy laugh. I string thread around these solid pegs, weaving my own picture. Getting too close to these men dissolves the mirage and dissipates the longing. More pegs rise up, the thread slips off, and an unstable tangle falls into my cupped hand. The men I've longed for, they loved every volume of Knausgaard's *My Struggle*, refused to kiss after sex, persisted in believing they were smarter than me (even when given ample evidence to the contrary). *How silly*, I thought, *you are not who I made you to be.* I know this, know that space is necessary to sustain this kind of desire, so I try to preserve the distance. I don't ask too many questions, not *Where were you born?* or *What are your parents like?* or *Are you as fucked up as I am?* I stay quiet. Longing is built on emptiness, and this absence appeals to me. It's why I'm so comfortable with longing; pining is an isolating experience.

My longing looks like this: moony hours staring out windows, imagining conversations, interactions, sometimes just the face of my desired. Agonizing over crafting a witty response to a message, tweaking sentences in my head as I spoon breakfast granola into my mouth, then fretting over my words until the object of my desire writes back. I smile reflexively when my phone buzzes with their name. Walking to class, having a drink, I'll turn to a friend, "What do you think he means?" (Reader: they always mean exactly what they say.) My desire feels urgent, like the next second is the most important one, my body buzzing, humming with stalled momentum, but from the outside, longing mostly looks like blocks of time devoted to a distant person.

Desire fixes me in amber, perpetually holding me at arm's length, no further, no closer. Time seems to stop because there is no movement. This pleases me, stopping time. Grief, of course, seals off time too. When he died, I was thrown into a different dimension while my body remained in this one, this dimension that was empty of my dad, this dimension where I had no one to call when I heard Talking Heads on the radio, where the house didn't smell like boxed brownies, where I didn't fall asleep to the sound of someone reading aloud *A Brief History of Time*, this dimension that was empty.

In the silver car, driving down streets draped with oak trees, I look over at Dad. He is on the cusp of needing to shave again. If I reach out to touch his five o'clock shadow, I know it will feel prickly. When he kisses my cheek some mornings, I feel it, a roughness scratching my face. Outside, it is another Carolina day: hot, humid, dripping like butter. I take a deep breath, getting ready to speak. It's the type of question I feel self-conscious asking; I'm old enough to recognize how earnest it is and young enough to be embarrassed by that. Still, I want to know. "Dad," I say, looking at his profile, his hands at ten and two on the cracked steering wheel, "what's the meaning of life?" He smiles. I can tell he's thought this over, a pearl worried smooth by a small piece of grit. "I don't think there is a meaning to life," he says, "but I think we make life meaningful." He means through love. He means we make life meaningful through love.

I believe him. I will believe him for years. I will never stop believing him. That becomes the problem. I mean: How is life supposed to have meaning without him? How am I supposed to go on wanting the world when he is gone?

In general, I prefer to be the person longed for rather than the one doing the longing. At the start of summer, I met a man with long hair and an ultralight bike at a bar. We had one beer, maybe two, and talked about music and get-rich-quick schemes. Then, I left the state for the summer, flew thousands of miles away, yet he continued to text me all season long, inviting me to coffee, to concerts, over to his place where he was making pizza with his neighbors and where I could meet his big, fluffy dog. I sometimes responded and sometimes didn't. On my birthday, I danced and kissed a different man who would pine for me for over half a year, though I never saw him again. And once, a man with completely opposite political views pursued me for years, meeting me for quick lunches, making excuses to visit my roommates, offering me basketball tickets he'd promised to friends. But listen: it's not about these men; it's about me. It's not about these men; it's about desire.

I understand how to be desirable. Some of it is in looks, sure, a bare shoulder, Mona Lisa smile, eyes that linger half a beat too long, but that's all surface level; true longing lies deeper. Here's a trick: let slip one deeply personal, mundane thing. *I try olives once every five years because I wish I loved them, but I never do.* Or *the smell of honeysuckle reminds me of how we used to pinch off the petals and lick the innards when we were kids.* Or *I haven't been to church since he died.* Then, vanish. Become elusive. A glimmering void, a black hole no one can enter or escape.

I enjoy dwelling in absence, and this penchant lends itself well to longing. It must be clear why this is, why I am good at being gone—it brings me closer to my dad. I started learning how to be absent after he died. It was easy. What did it matter who asked me to prom? Who touched my thigh? Who kissed my neck? I detached from this world, wanting to be closer to a different one. When I mimic his absence, we are once again in the same place: gone. In grief, aloofness comes naturally, and men are apt to fall for a phantom.

Most people have bikes downtown (it's faster than walking and easier than parking a car), but I prefer my feet; I like walking places alone, spending time in my head and hyperfocused on the world around me: the smell of Sonoran hotdogs, the sound of drunken chatter chirping above loud music, the feel of concrete thick and hard beneath my thin-souled shoes. He rides a bike, though.

We've had a nice dinner and listened to music and drunk a beer, and now it's late. As he unlocks his bike, I look around. Girls wear gold-chain necklaces and boys walk a half-step behind them. Some of the neon signs blink, and their light obscures the buildings behind them. It smells like cigarette smoke, and everything wears the gauze of it. I feel removed, separate. When he pulls his bike in front of me, I force a half-smile. He's on the edge of saying something too honest; I can see it in his big pupils and parted lips. I can't take it. I cut him off. "Bye," I say, and I don't look back, just step into the night, and keep walking.

"Absence becomes an active practice, a *business* (which keeps me from doing anything else)," writes Barthes. Absence needs tending. A garden: water it, prune it, cover it in winter. Weed it, till it, turn the field over. Wake up early, go to bed late. There's nothing passive about absence; you must work to keep it alive.

My favorite book the year my dad died was Salinger's

Franny and Zooey. I used to carry it around in a cheap imitation leather satchel. The bag was cracking, and the book's cover creased in odd places. It was my amulet, though at the time, I couldn't put into words why. Looking back, I recognize it had everything to do with Franny's preoccupation with the Jesus prayer. She explains, "If you keep saying that prayer over and over again—you only have to just do it with your lips at first—then eventually what happens, the prayer becomes self-active. Something happens after a while. I don't know what, but something happens, and the words get synchronized with the person's heartbeats, and then you're actually praying without ceasing." I became obsessed with this idea, with the idea that if you said something enough, if you repeated it out loud over and over again, that eventually, if you said it enough, your body would never stop saying it. Stories became physical, incarnate.

The thing these men failed to realize is that my body is a Jesus prayer for grief, for loss, for my dad. Because they missed my body's truth, they never truly touched me. They made it easy to disappear. On my couch, with our bare feet propped up on the coffee table, a man asked me if I believed in God. "I don't know," I said, "but after my Dad died, I started believing in something. I can't believe he's just gone." The man cringed. At a restaurant, over expensive street tacos dripping with spicy aioli, a man told me he liked going to funerals because it made him reevaluate his life. "Do you want to keep talking about this?" I asked. He replied, "Why not?" He'd forgotten my dad was dead. On the banks of the Thames, sitting on a bench as the dark water slapped the channel, a man tried to hug me when I said, "I take after my dad, but he died." I pushed his hug aside, kissed him instead. I wanted to keep the distance between us. I wanted desire, not love. He couldn't understand the abyss I lived in. He couldn't understand that every morning I woke up devastated my dad was still dead, couldn't understand that every cell in my body called out to him. No, he couldn't understand me, so I let desire unfurl the distance between us. This man, all these men, they knew nothing about the depth of my desire. How could they?

The plastic casing warps open, and the scent of white rose blooms. The petals are chilled and soft, fragile in my hand, but I'm worried about sticking him with the boutonnière's pin. I can feel him watching me pull at his lapel, his eyes skimming over the braids my cousin worked around the crown of my head, slipping past my darkened eyelashes, settling on my fidgeting hands. "I don't think I'm doing this right," I laugh, and my cousin steps in to help pin it. Mom and Dad stand five paces away, smiling across the distance. Once my corsage is tight around my wrist, Dad takes pictures of me and my date with his bulky Nikon, the one he snaps at soccer games to give his hands something to do. My date's hand lands light on my back, and I don't know if I should lean into the distance, so I freeze, and we keep an awkward half inch between us. I'm embarrassed, of course. Too young to know how to hide myself without physical distance, so as more people crowd around the backyard, girls smoothing satin and chiffon, boys pulling at cummerbunds, my date and I allow ourselves to drift apart. He stands by the fishpond with his best friend, both of them propping one foot on the stone edge.

Mom, Dad, and I lilt toward the corner of the yard, away from everyone else. My cousin takes the camera from Dad as we huddle in front of the garden gate. It's the only picture the three of us will take tonight, one of the last pictures in which Dad will look healthy. I stand in between them and hold Dad's waist so tightly that my corsage disappears into the loose fabric of his button-down. I hold him so tightly that his arm eases up in surprise, like a bird startled into flight. I hold him so tightly that I fool myself into thinking I can keep him here, that I can tether him to me.

You took my breath away, caught my eye, stole my heart. I was blinded by love and shot through the heart. Common idioms concur: longing takes something from us. The object of our desire holds a piece of us, a hand, an ear, the skin on our back. This is nothing new. Anne Carson, in *Eros: The Bittersweet*, collects a slew of similar sayings from classical Greek poetry: "A hole is being gnawed in [my] vitals," "you have snatched the lungs out of my chest" and "pierced me right through the bones," "you have worn me down," "grated me away," "devoured my flesh," "sucked my blood," "mowed off my genitals," and "stolen my reasoning mind." Since ancient times, we've recognized that desire physically wounds us (for what is a wound but an absence where body should be?). The desired pries a piece of us from our body, and I wonder if we can ever get any of ourselves back, if we even want back the parts of us that have been stolen. Look at me, wandering around with skinned knees and scratched arms, my chest flayed open; I'm a walking wound, leaving blood like breadcrumbs behind me.

Wine and tulip beer glasses hang above our heads, glittering while they cup the open air. I eat my cheese flatbread and stare at the silver taps in front of me. He's talking about his wife, who he's been separated from for years but still loves; he's talking about another woman, who he cares for but doesn't know in what way; he's trying to say he doesn't want me anymore. My flatbread tastes greasy. I feel it coating my stomach in oil. I keep eating it, looking at the silver taps, watching the bartender flip them open and shut. When the man has tired himself out talking, I look at him. His glasses have clear frames, so I can see his whole face: smeared with freckles and sun. He's over half a decade older than me, but he's always struck me as younger, more earnest. "I'm seeing other people," I say. "Oh,"

he says, "that makes this easier." I flag down the bartender and ask for a to-go box.

Outside, it's sunny and hot, a dry heat, so it feels both oppressive and empty. With the thin cardboard container in my hands, I start to cry. I feel like a gutted fish, slit down the belly, all my organs pulled out. It's not that I lost him but that I realize I've lost so much of myself. I pull my phone out but don't know who to call, or I do, but I can't. It's not possible anymore. He's gone. I take a deep breath, let the air fill my lungs before they empty back out.

Meleager, a poet from the first century BCE, writes, "Pain has begun to touch my heart, for hot Love, / as he strayed, scratched it with the tip of his nails, / and, smiling, said, 'Again, O unhappy lover, thou / shalt have the sweet wound, burnt by biting honey.'" Love claws open your heart and leaves behind desire, that "sweet wound."

I consider my wounds. At a bar, when I mentioned financial inheritance and someone said, "That must be nice. Some distant relative, huh?" In the kitchen with chilaquiles frying, when someone rolled their eyes at the ultrawhite tennis shoes their dad wore. In another country, when I asked a sweaty guitarist his name and he answered back my dad's. His absence is everywhere, and it hurts, of course it hurts, but it tastes sweet, too. Walking by a stone church, I remember in the pews, how he would elbow me and sing, "All things dull and ugly, all creatures short and squat." Checking the shower temperature, I remember how he flung water at me, tricked me into thinking it was from the toilet. Spreading a restaurant's napkin across my lap, I remember our placemats at home. They were wooden rods woven together and dyed bright colors. After a few years of use, they became faded from summer suppers on the porch, so Dad and I went to the store to buy new ones, but we didn't tell Mom. At home, we threw away the old ones and left the new ones soaking in the sink for Mom to see. "Oh my goodness," she said, "how did you get these clean? I scrubbed and scrubbed, but they never came clean." "Windex," I said, and Dad smiled. "This one's even a different color, but it looks so clean!" she said. We let her praise Windex for a few hours before we told her the truth. Years later, at the restaurant, unfolding my napkin, I smile.

Absence is an opening, a hole you can drop through. The thirteenth-century poet Rumi says, "The wound is the place where the Light enters you." When I talk about my wounds, the spots scraped empty inside me, I'm not just talking about pain; no, I'm also saying, *Look. Look how much I can hold.*

The open pocket door lets light in, reflections from the bathroom bouncing filtered sun into the closet. Mom's shoes have overflowed her own closet, sandals and slip-ons leaving only a semicircle of space open in Dad's closet. I stand in it. It's quiet, like someone has stuffed cotton balls in my ears. I don't hear the AC whirring or the dog scampering downstairs or the lawn mower humming next door—I only hear the room itself. When I step forward, finding a patch of floor between the shoes, my legs groan from my morning run. They ache. My hands skim his shirts, feeling the starch of checkered button-downs, the stiffness of red plaid, and the raised patches of his troop master uniform. I pull on the sleeve of blue batik shirt.

Yellow, pink, and purple salamanders crawl over the navy background. The lines aren't crisp but blurred, blue dye cutting through the bodies of some creatures, dots of yellow and pink spackling the shirt elsewhere. I remember this shirt. He wore it on a Florida vacation, and I had a matching dress. *Cut from the same cloth,* as they say. In my mind, we are on the beach in the early evening. The bugs are out, and the sun is low. My skin is warm from the day's heat and my cheeks are pink with glee as I run into his arms. He scoops me up and carries me away. I tug on the shirt's sleeve. It's now, when I start to cry, that I realize I've been smiling.

The shirt has been worn soft, and I push my face into the thin fabric. It smells smooth and musky, like moss and soap, like a day well spent, like him. I grab up more of the fabric, rub my face into it, bury my nose, my mouth, my whole head. I keep pushing against it like it can break open into another world, forcing my nose, my face, my skin into the fibers. I smother myself like it's the only way I can breathe because it's the only way I can breathe. When I pull back, I drop the shirt and empty out my lungs. How sweet it is, this pain.

METHODICAL TENDERNESS

1. GUIDE RAILS

I held out for as long as I could, letting my windshield Jackson-Pollock interstate bugs, bodies turned to splatters, layers of dirt building over the hot metal hood. My windows even stopped working: I'd roll them down, then have to pinch and pull them back up, fingerprints dimpling the glass like clouds crowding the sky. It made drive-throughs and paid parking garages and driving anywhere in the early Arizona summer unbearable. My brother convinced me to go to the carwash. "The dirt is getting stuck in the mechanism," he said, "that's why your windows don't work." He explained that the external had broken the internal. I didn't always trust him, but he was an engineer, and I needed someone to depend on.

2. ENTRY EYES

We live three time zones apart, my brother and I, and that makes sense to me. I'm a writer; he's dyslexic. He's an engineer; I can't conceive of months as numbers. There's always been a lag in our relationship, telephone lines slack between us, communication slow and understanding even slower. We broke apart in different ways. We're still learning to care for each other, to see each other clearly, cleanly.

3. PRE-SOAK ARCH

Will lives in rural South Carolina, where hay bales and rustic crosses sprout along the winding roads, not far from where he went to college, his life tied down in complicated knots. Dad died in early August, and Will went to college later that month. Brick walkways and buildings mapped onto rolling hills. Open fields surrounded sporadic dorms, and orange shirts swamped the campus every Friday during football season. Will reached out to other students, wanting friendship and connection, just someone to spend time with, really, but the men, some familiar and some new, clammed at the first sign of vulnerability. They didn't know what to say; they didn't know they only needed to listen. I will never forgive them for this, for the ways they taught my brother to lock everything inside himself. He grew an opaque rind and hid his tenderness within, skin concealing viscera. No one could see what lay beneath. I remember visiting him for a football game in college. There's a picture of me, Mom, and Will smiling in the concrete bowl of a stadium, Death Valley. But the photo only captures the surface; I felt acutely out of place, an observer, a witness to the game, to the visit, to my brother. I could feel the distance yawn between us. Years later, when I stay with him in his new oversize home, I watch his grief crack through in anger. He gets an email offering Dad a new job in Washington, and he tracks down the hospital associated with the application so he can send them an email telling them to get a new hiring staff. "Will, it might not be their fault," I say, leaning my elbows on his kitchen counter. "It could be the database." He stands on the opposite side of the island, upright. "They're trying to hire a dead doctor," he says, tone lowered to a growl. I say nothing but push back from the cool counter. "I've already had this conversation with someone else," he says. I turn to leave the room and say, "Then we don't need to have it again." He tries to pick a fight, and I walk away.

4. TIRE AND WHEEL APPLICATOR

I live in Arizona, a scroll of land populated with cacti and adobe homes, a place where no one knows my dad except me. I don't know who to talk to about how the oddly adapted flowers remind me of the Dr. Suess books he used to read to me, about how the punk music spilling into the streets reminds me of his records, about how a cool drink in the hell-bent heat reminds me of the summers we spent outside. I don't know what to say, so mostly, I don't say anything. The last time Will visited me, I was short-circuiting, sobbing every day, though I didn't know why. In the car, on the couch, walking up hiking trails pitted with saguaros, I cried. When Dad died, I was in high school, and though I didn't know how to ask for help, everyone knew I needed it. It was a small school, one where the same faces surrounded me from nursery to twelfth grade, where everyone saw Dad in the cold metal stands at soccer games, where it was okay for me to leave French class and come back with puffy eyes. *J'ai pleuré, je pleure, je vais pleurer.* I was a doll: pull my string for tears. It's a defense mechanism still lodged in my system. It brings people in but keeps a pane of distance between us. You can see what's inside me, but you can't touch it. How can anyone understand this grief? When Will visited, I couldn't stop crying, and he didn't know what to say. There was nothing to say. Still, he followed me out of Mexican restaurants to put a heavy hand on my shoulder, handed over cash for our powdered breakfast pastries, and made me chocolate chip cookies while I laid in bed watching *The Office.* He tried to look beneath the crying, to see what it meant, what that kind of brokenness signaled; he tried to see how to fix it. He's an engineer at heart, too. At the end of his visit, when I dropped him off at the airport, he gave me a folded twenty, a ten, and four ones with a neon pink sticky note saying "Mister Carwash, Platinum Wash." I rolled my eyes. "My car is dirty because I've been driving you around all week," I said. He said nothing. I took the cash, we hugged, and he left.

5. TOP WASHER

I drive Dad's car now, a sleek silver SUV that looks kin to a minivan and indeed was a soccer caravan for many years. The car wheel wells are splattered with dirt, and Dad's old parking sticker, a bull's-eye centered on the license plate, has begun to crack off in the sun. The windows are so dusty bored teenagers might well write "wash me" with their fingers on its back. It's clear: the car is dirty, and I know I should go to the car wash, but I don't. I don't because I don't want to go to the car wash; I don't want a clean car; I don't want it to look new. I want to see the car's history plainly on its face. I want to look at it and see Dad driving down backcountry roads, his hands at ten and two, his eyes checking the rearview to see my brother and me sprawling in the back, our soccer cleats cratering the carpet, grass and dirt matting into its fibers, sweat slicking the leather seats. I want to look at it and see Dad slicing the car through sea-salt air, his hair warbling under the open sunroof, sand stippling his hairy legs, trailer hitched with secondhand jet skis and sun-bleached life vests jumbled in the trunk. I want to look at it and see Dad slurping the dregs of a Rush's milkshake, look at it and smell the toasted cheeseburger bun, hear the CD player stumble to the next song, hear Talking Heads pining for home.

6. TIRE BRUSH

Two nights before Dad died, as Mom and I drove back from the hospital in the collapsing light of day, I threw up on the side of that silver car, rolled down the window and let the nothing that I'd eaten come out. The wind from the road felt cool against my face, and Mom touched the small of my back from the driver's seat while I held my own hair. Vomit smeared itself across the door. It was grainy and full of bile. Will was on a pre-college camping trip, a leadership program meant to connect him with other people who enjoyed the outdoors. Maybe, at that moment, as I retched over the seatbelt of a moving car, he was setting up his tent, extending the poles, clicking them together, looping them through the thin fabric of a home, a home he'd take down and pack up the next day. Earlier, in the hospital room, Mom and I tracked down different phone numbers, writing them down on the back of an old receipt, trying to find someone who could tell my brother he needed to come home, some stranger who could tell him his dad was dying, soon. As we left for the night, Mom leaned down to Dad, told him he just needed to wait for Will, just one more night. The next morning, before light broke open, before Mom and I drove to the hospital, before Will was back, before he threw open the door of a moving car, before he stumbled toward us, T-shirt rumpled and hair uncombed, before he put his arms around Mom and me, before I leaned into the embrace like a plant in need of support, before the three of us walked into the hospital room spilled with light, before we were together, before it happened, before Dad died, in the cold dark of early day, I took a wet Clorox wipe to the silver car. I didn't want to clean up my insides, and the dried grit was sandpaper to my hand.

7. FLEX WRAPS AND SIDE WASHERS

On his twenty-sixth birthday, Will was quiet. I was in grad school and home for the summer, so I could celebrate with him, but we didn't have dinner reservations, so Will, Mom, and I sat at the bar of an upscale Southern restaurant, the kind that overcharged for grits and fried green tomatoes. The bar was stained dark, and a ring of coolant ran through it, keeping our beers and cocktails cold. "Are you okay?" Mom kept asking Will. "I'm fine," he'd say, blinking unnaturally. I suggested we start with oysters, and Mom said, "Your father made me try them every which way: raw, cooked, fried. I never liked them." I ordered twelve and they came on round metal trays with each shell cradled in a divot. The silver platters were dull, and the restaurant's dimmed lights showed scratches in their centers. The oysters looked luminous, almost transparent in their shells. I let the rough back rest in my palm, loosened the soft animal, and slurped. The meat slid down my throat, and I could've traced its slow progress with a finger. Mouth, pharynx, esophagus, stomach. The digestion was procedural in a way I could track. Will watched a muted TV as he worked on his oysters, and I watched him, then turned to Mom. "You have to try one," I said. "For Dad." She picked up the shell closest to her, the one with the smallest lump of meat, and pried the body loose with a fork. Will and I watched her sip from the shell. Her lips puckered, and she shook her head. Will laughed. The next morning, he washed the cars. As he unrolled the hose and set out the soap, I wonder if he remembered sitting in a cold AP environmental science classroom, a year before I sat there, two years before Dad died, and learning that if we control our environment, we have a better chance of survival. As he let the water cascade over the windows, blurring the car's vision, did he let it wash him back to that bright classroom, sun sinking its teeth through the windows? Did he remember penciling in his notes that if we control the variables, account for our surroundings, then we can focus on what's wrong, murky, misplaced?

8. UNDERCARRIAGE APPLICATOR

When Will was a senior in high school, he and Dad built a solar-electric hybrid car. It was as impressive as it sounds. Wearing dark face shields and thick gloves, they huddled in the garage, watching sparks shoot out and die as they welded together a four-wheeler's metal frame. They sat on the ground, eating white bread sandwiches and drinking cold sodas during their breaks, the smell of electric blue paint hanging in the air as another coat dried on metal. Like the Flintstone's car, there was no floor, but below both the passenger's and driver's seat, they affixed bicycle pedals and hung greased chains between the axles. As the evening settled in, they fiddled with the steering, turning the handlebars, left and right and left. A solar panel was fastened on top as the roof, and a nest of wires coiled around the motor behind the driver's seat like a tangle of neurons. It took them months to finish, and while they worked through each day and came in for supper sweat soaked and tired, I think they both would've liked the building process to last forever. In the end, "Will Power," the name Mom gave the car, was road tested and safety approved, which felt like a loose term to me because though it was equipped with seatbelts, I didn't feel very safe pedaling around the neighborhood without doors when a big SUV whooshed past. When Will left for college, he left the car behind. It's still in Mom's backyard. When she threatens to throw it away, he always says he'll take it, but there's never any follow-up. I don't think he can face it anymore. The wheels are flat, and the solar panel was stripped for another project. Riddled with leaves, the car's body rusts in the shade of a big pecan tree.

9. RINSE ARCH

Whenever we stop for gas, Will cleans the car's windshield. The asphalt is stuck with blackened gum, and neon signs advertising beer glow in the windows. It smells like dust and gasoline. He steps out of the truck or out of my faux van or out of Mom's car with one tennis-shoed foot turned out further than the other, a hip dysplasia Dad diagnosed years ago. On the soccer field, it was how I picked Will out: his gait. In the stands, I picked Dad out by his voice. When he got loud, it thinned, warbling at the end like jet-plane trails. I wonder if Will remembers how Dad yelped when Will headed the ball into the back of the net, putting a playoff game into overtime. It was his only goal in high school. Dad hooped and hollered, shaking the metal stands, and they reverberated back with pride. He beamed down at the green field, at Will. Truthfully though, Dad was always that proud of him.

10. WAX ARCH

Beside the car, Will glides the squeegee across the pimpled windshield, letting the dirt mix with water before he paints another row below. He takes his time, never missing an inch of the glass's face. There's love in the attention he gives the task, a methodical tenderness in the way he cares for cars. His orange T-shirt or his blue polo pulls against his body, and he might push his baseball hat back on his head (so he can see better) or wipe sweat from his hairline. I watch his hands grip the squeegee's black handle, his fingernails ragged and small, lined with dirt. Dad's nails were always short, too. He'd bite them down, a habit I inherited from him. To stop myself, I paint my nails dark green, deep red, or light blue, these flakes of color an attempt to keep from externalizing my anxiety. I prefer to stow my feelings inside myself, to keep the hood shut over my rattling engine, though I'm trying to change this, to not be ashamed of the ways my innards are broken, to let others touch my throbbing hangnails and pull. I imagine offering my hand—nails bitten and all—to Will, head down, timid. He would hold a digit gingerly, rotate it, his breath warm on my infected finger while he inspected the tender skin.

11. SPOT-FREE ARCH

Once one half of the windshield is wet, Will swirls the squeegee in his warm hand, flipping it to the other side. He sets the rubber flap against the glass and takes his time, pulling with care, lining each new row up with the one above it like a careful shave. From inside the car, I watch the water unzip itself from glass. The squeegee squeals from friction. At the end of one row, Will flicks the excess water onto the ground, more wetness waiting to evaporate. He keeps pulling until half the glass is clean, his arms taut, muscles moving skin, and then, he loosens, lets his body relax until he lumbers to the other side and paints another row. He never looks up. It's a meditation: I can see the stillness inside him, a calmness created by cleaning the surface. A transparent outside means you can better see into the inside, means you can see from the inside out. At home, when he's starting a new project, he lays everything out, nuts and bolts in separate plastic cups, diagrams unfolded before him. His thoughts are manifest physically. When he works, there isn't a barrier between what's inside his head and what's around him, but I prefer to keep the two separate. My work is writing, and I write the things I can't say. It's always been this way. When I was a child, my parents would find folded-up sheets of notebook paper on their pillows at night, apologies I didn't know how to verbalize. It was the only type of communication where I felt comfortable being honest. I wrote those notes alone, without another body present, but I understood that writing was a belief in an absent reader. So, I wrote the things inside me that I couldn't speak. What I didn't realize back then, what Will learned over the years, what I am still learning now, is that it's impossible to separate the two: cleaning the car's exterior actually preserves its interior mechanisms, something I didn't understand until my windows began to stick.

12. TIRE GLAZE

At the end of Will's visit, he hands me folded cash with a pink sticky note on top. The bills feel thin in damp hands, the sticky note crisp. It's midday and there are no clouds in the sky, no breeze, just heat. The airport is ground level, so the emptiness hovers above us, daring us to look up. Will's baseball cap shields his eyes, and my oversize sunglasses slip down my nose. I can't say thank you because I'm not thankful. Because shouldn't Dad be reminding me to clean the car? Shouldn't he be calling to ask how our visit went? Shouldn't we be annoyed at his intrusion in our relationship? And yet that's what we have now: our dad, missing between us. We navigate around the absence, chiseling out the shape, coming closer and closer to naming it, coming closer and closer to embracing it. Will takes his bag out of the car and looks at me, eyes shaded beneath the bill of his hat. He pulls at the hem of his T-shirt, and I tuck a stray hair behind my ear. We stall because neither of us likes leavings. We're exposed. When we finally hug, he feels warm, larger than he used to be, larger than me, solid and safe, if only for now.

13. AIR DRYERS WITH FIN NOZZLE

A few weeks later, I go to the car wash. My windows still aren't working, but I'm too embarrassed to open the car door to talk to the attendant, so I roll down the driver's side window, knowing it will be a pain to pull back up. After paying the jump-suited man, passing him the cash my brother pressed into my hands and selecting the wash option he wrote on a sticky note, I drive into the car wash's mouth, slowly, pulling the window up manually as I roll into the shadows. I tug with the spindly muscles in my arms. When I'm swallowed by the structure, I turn the AC down, and the white noise vanishes. "Relax and enjoy the ride," a prerecorded voice says. I sit up in my leather seat, sweat coating the backsides of my thighs, and the car lurches forward. A man manually sprays the windshield with water and suds, coating what he can of the exterior before the track pulls me forward. Blood gallops through my veins. The water carries memories. When I was little, Mom and Dad took me and Will to the car wash as a treat, thinking we would love the razzle dazzle of it. Will was mesmerized by the water and suds, fascinated by the mechanics of the cleaning, but I screamed and didn't stop crying till we left. I felt like I was drowning. Years later, the same irrational fear wells up in me.

Or maybe it's a new one, maybe it's the residue of a sharp memory, my hand against the car's body, wiping vomit off the door. Either way, in the car wash, I feel out of control. Blue, pink, and yellow soap suds spit onto the hood of my car, and strips of blue cloth, like the heavy head of a drenched mop, flick it off. The fabric whaps the glass; it sounds strong enough to crack the windshield. For a moment, there are no suds and no fabric, and I can look around at the mechanical mouth, peeking through the droplets and bulky machinery at the oddly dingy walls. They seem so ordinary, dirty and hung with tools like my brother's garage, and this calms me. But the view disappears quickly once the "Hot Shine" portion of the wash, complete with red-heat lights, pours a blanket of magma-like foam over the car. There's a spectacle about the carwash, meant to distract from the practicality, the chore-like nature of washing the car, but the bigness just makes me feel small. I feel trapped. I never feel claustrophobic except in car washes, but as more fabric combs the car, I have nothing to do but sit with myself and watch the wash clean my car. I try to feel less compressed and more embraced. Water drips over the car, over me. Industrial strength air dryers shake the car's frame, and then the tunnel opens. I see the world again: the saguaros emblematic of this state so far from home, the dusty roads pockmarked with potholes filled with sand, the other cars on their way to other lives, through their other lives. My car, my dad's car, will get dirty again in a matter of weeks, maybe days, but for now, it glistens, the metal and the windshield made clear, made clean. I roll down the window, but it still won't roll back up. Of course, some damage can't be undone. I laugh and text my brother.

THE SKY COME DOWN

*S*ometimes it surprises me. The sudden plop-plop of big drops like penny after penny in a wishing well; the taste of fresh soil a mouthful I wasn't expecting. Mostly, though, I know it's coming. It announces itself as the ache in my knees when I stand up, the sun slinking away, the thunder rolling. It starts as pins dropping, needles slipped into haystacks. The concrete is pitted, then covered. The grass is slick. The water snaps its fingers, claps, yells. The water won't stop coming.

After Dad died, I fell in love with the rain, though I didn't initially recognize how this loss and love were connected. There was something in the way these two opposites coalesced that drew me closer, but I couldn't name why or how. For a while, I couldn't even say that it was this splitness that called to me. All I knew was that when it rained, I felt at home.

During the day, running errands or walking to class, I'd turn my face up to meet it, catch the drops in my mouth and let the water fill my cupped hands. Other people hurried with their heads down, huddling beneath umbrellas and pulling their jackets tight, but I clomped in my bright blue rain boots, seeking out the deepest puddles and splashing through the length of them. Sometimes I kicked so high, the water slipped into my boots and soaked my socks. I didn't care; in class, my feet brined in rainwater, grapes wrinkling to raisins. Heading home, I'd pull down my rain jacket's hood and let the rain dampen my hair and freckle my cheeks. A seed breaking through its shell, poking through the dirt, unfurling its stem; how glorious to feel alive.

Of course, I knew rain's dangers too. On what would have been my dad's fifty-fifth birthday, my hometown flooded. Over twenty inches of rain pelted the city, and the river overtook land. The tax building bent like a supplicant, the vet's office bloated, and water filled homes to the brim. The interstate was impassable, and local roads collapsed. Firefighters rescued people evacuating from their cars. My mom, thankfully, was visiting my brother upstate, and my dad had been dead for three years. I urgently texted friends still in town: they were alive. News anchors called it the "thousand-year flood," and the damage is still there. Some homes were never returned to; some people never came back. In total, the water killed nineteen people.

One of two things happens when you drown: you breathe in water, or you don't breathe at all. A drowning victim, after struggling to keep their head above water (often hyperventilating while flailing), will hold their breath once submerged. As oxygen levels drop and carbon dioxide levels climb, the body begs for breath. The mouth opens, and water rushes in. When it reaches the throat, the larynx, that strong muscle lining the neck, seizes. It keeps water out of the lungs, but the body still needs oxygen, and it can't breathe if the throat is closed. Systems begin to click off. Nerves, muscles, vision. The heart might continue until the larynx releases and water surges in, filling the lungs and collapsing the alveoli (the air sacs that exchange carbon dioxide for oxygen). Or the heart could stop before that, and the throat might never open. It doesn't much matter: in the end, you drown.

When my dad was twenty-four, he almost drowned. He was in Alaska for his OB/GYN rotation, helping to bring tens of babies into the world, but when he had time off, he preferred to spend it beneath wide open skies. In Denali National Park, Dad and his friend followed a river until it pinched in and thinned out like a waist. They carried bulky backpacks that clinked with tent poles, tins of food, and lightweight flashlights. The river ran clean, and the air smelled of spruce. Flocks of snow buntings warbled nearby. In the water, Dad took one step at a time, planting his foot in the riverbed and bracing against the current before swiveling his hips and pivoting his back leg forward. He made it halfway before the water swept him under. The current was quicker, stronger than he realized. His body pummeled downstream. His backpack pushed his head underwater. He couldn't get his footing. He couldn't breathe. His friend couldn't help, and Dad would've died if his foot hadn't snagged on land, if he hadn't been able to turn his head to air.

Of all weather-related disasters, floods are the deadliest, and it's no surprise that in floods most people die by drowning. All that water, so little land. In the span of twelve years, thirty-two floods killed 1,185 people in the United States, almost all of them through drowning. That's roughly three and a half Boeing 747s nosediving into the ocean; imagine the wreckage. Floods can come on quickly, relentlessly, violently, and they're often brought on by heavy rain.

The first flood story I ever heard fits the bill. In Sunday school, sitting in a plastic chair that was a little too small with a paper cup of lemonade and a napkin full of goldfish, I learned Noah's tale. Sun-drenched, Noah cut, carved, and sanded wood. He looked foolish, building an ark on dry land, a massive boat so far from water, but God had told him, only him, that the flood was coming. He worked every day, tiring his body out, and woke up the next morning to do it all over again.

His muscles ached. Maybe he suffered lacerations from saws or puncture wounds from nails. Regardless, he kept working. Then, one day, it was time. He climbed aboard his handmade boat, ushered on his family, and guided the preordained pairs of animals onto the ark. Rain slicked their hides and dripped from their noses. It flung from swinging tails and slipped off bent backs. For forty days and forty nights, the rain fell.

The bible's book of Genesis (meaning "generation," "creation") recounts God's destructive rains. In the beginning, God separated the "waters above earth" from those below to let the land rise and dry, inflammation swelling up around a wound. Animals drew their limbs together, grazing on grass, munching on trees, a pleasant pastoral, but eventually humans fucked it all up with their sins and God got angry. He wanted to punish the earth. For forty days and forty nights, God slid open the "windows of heaven" and let the water from above return to itself below, drowning the world anew. Land vanished, along with everything on it. After one hundred and fifty days, God remembered Noah, and the water receded. The world was mud and bones, a graveyard of muck. The flood wiped out the majority of the population, killed almost all the creatures who once inhabited earth, and yet, in the end, Noah arrived at a beginning, not an end. The world started over with survivors as its seed. In that makeshift classroom in that drafty church, the same church that would host my dad's funeral years later, where I would sweat through a stiff black dress in the front pew, where I would sniffle snot back up my nose, where I would weep so deeply my rib cage knocked itself sore, in that same church, I heard some of the first stories I was ever told, and I learned, early on, that a rebirth requires death.

The paradoxical nature of rain, its creative and destructive prowess, permeates literature. William Faulkner's rain in *As I Lay Dying* is "big as buckshot," while James Joyce's *Dubliners*

finds "the fine incessant needles of water playing in the sodden beds." In Virginia Woolf's *The Years*, it's "peppering the pavements and making them greasy," but for Jesmyn Ward in *Sing, Unburied, Sing*, "the sky dumps water on the tin roof of the building." Elizabeth Hardwick's *Sleepless Nights'* rain places the "the solace of opening the door and finding everyone there" next to "the cemetery wait[ing] to be desecrated," and in *Kafka on the Shore*, Haruki Murakami compares the "stinging pain of rain" to a "religious initiation." The rain is big and fine, peppering and dumping, revitalizing and useless, painful and exultant. Underneath these texts, there's a similar biblical current for me, one that shows that water is as cleansing as it is damaging, and this current, this sense of rain as savior and conqueror, pulls me to heaven and hell, to my undergraduate English degree, and, ultimately, to John Milton.

My copy of Milton's *Complete Poems and Major Prose* had a navy cover and a cloth spine that came unglued on one side. It was thicker than a brick, and two days a week I lugged it to class, where I sat in a semicircle and discussed the dialectical nature of *Paradise Lost* and *Paradise Regained*. The dialectic, we learned, was when opposites synthesized. It's not that one force collapses beneath the other; rather, the friction between them moves them both into a third, integrated state. For example, Milton wrote, "both ends of Heav'n, the Clouds / From many a horrid rift abortive pour'd / Fierce rain and lightning mixt, water with fire / In ruine reconcil'd." Here, water and fire, rain and lightning, are the opposites, and the third state they settle into is ruin.

The dialectic in my own life is clear: I am alive and my dad is not. I listen to the new Fleet Foxes album, and my dad does not. I eat too much double crème brie, and he cannot. I wake up in the morning, and he is dead. Every moment, every movement in my life is paired with the dark absence in his. These two truths feel incongruous, and yet they indisputably exist beside each other. I'm here; he isn't. These two opposites, my life and his death, friction into a new reality, and I'm no longer afraid to admit that I'm a ruin. Part of the old me eroded, and I was made new, damaged.

Grief dismantled me. I cried everywhere. In class, where I'd leave to go to the bathroom and fail to convince myself that cold water could soften my red and puffy eyes. Driving, where I'd have to squint through tears and measure out breaths so that I could see to get home safely (this did not always work; I once backed into a brick wall at my friend's house and permanently dented my bumper, shifting the shape of the wall). I cried over greasy cheeseburgers, on walks to the co-op with friends, in bed until I fell asleep, only to wake and start again. It was extravagant, this reaction; I knew it. I luxuriated in my pain. I refused to be quiet about it. Picture those houses warped by the flood, the ones still standing years later even though they're irreparably damaged. Their window screens are scratched open, their wood bloated and raw. They creak in the wind and smell of mold and mildew. I love those houses, the ones that refuse to be bulldozed, the ones that wear their trauma without shame. How beautiful and ghostly, how stunning, those ruins.

My own brand of ruin, weeping, is a type of devastation unique to humans. We're the only creatures who cry from emotional pain, though for centuries it wasn't clear why. The Bible's Old Testament suggests tears are produced when the heart is weakened and turned to water, and in the 1600s, Descartes, among others, hypothesized that feelings heated the heart, creating water vapor that condensed to tears and cooled the vital organ. It wasn't until 1662 that the lacrimal gland, the physiological origin of tears, was found, but even then, the investigation stopped at the mechanical: they could tell us how but not why.

Today, researchers speculate that emotional tears come from being overwhelmed, from feelings meeting a body and the two frictioning out a new precipitate. "Crying signals to yourself and other people that there's some important problem that is at least temporarily beyond your ability to cope," says

Jonathan Rottenberg, director of the Mood and Emotion Laboratory. He suggests that crying is a physical manifestation of emotional turmoil, that when we digest a truth our body cannot metabolize, we cry. Tears are feelings made physical.

❦

Dad and I used to watch the clouds. We'd lie on sticky grass and point out the shapes we saw in the sky. One arm tucked behind his head, Dad circled sailboats, monkeys, and castles above us. "See that one," he'd say, closing one eye, leaning his head against mine, "that one's a clown, with a big nose and painted mouth." "And a little hat!" I'd squeal. My body was a miniature of his, each of us with one leg bent and propped up. I squinted at the bright blue expanse, scrunching my nose so I could keep staring into the sky, searching out mountains chiseled by woodpeckers and pineapples seated next to giant squirrels. The breeze tickled our faces and cooled our arms. We let ourselves splay. Together we saw whole worlds in cumulous clouds. Superheroes, pelicans, soccer cleats, and mustachioed men. Blue whales, court jesters, fast cars, and flying fish. We passed entire afternoons this way, the two of us looking at the stories the sky offered us.

So is it any wonder I cried all the time? I loved my dad, and he loved me. Our lives were uncomplicated in a boring way: we were happy.

And then he got cancer.

And then he died.

And the foundations cracked open beneath me. I mean that the thing I trusted the most in the world, his love, vanished, overnight, and it wrecked me. The windows shattered, shards stuck like teeth in their frames. The wooden doors rotted though in holes and let the wind scream into the living room, howling every night. Pictures bruised with mold, and padded furniture atrophied. The walls buckled, and the roof collapsed. The mattress never completely dried. It was swift and unyielding, that violence. And yet, over the years, I learned to love what remained.

Ruins preserve the importance of the initial site and the process that damaged it. They contain themselves (now), their ghost selves (the ones that were destroyed), and the distance between them. Consider Machu Pichu, the Acropolis, Angkor Wat, Teotihuacan. Consider Pompeii, that ruin preserved and devastated by the volcanic ash that rained down on it. Today, the cobblestone streets are color leached, and brick walls stand solitary, enclosing nothing. The basilica's columns tense at attention, but the second story is now just sky. Volcanic debris knocked out much of the city, collapsing roofs and eroding homes, but it also preserved the remnants for centuries, protecting the city from the natural decay weather can bring. For years, no sun, wind, or rain touched it. The city weathered nothing after that destruction until its remains were dug up and out. The statue of Apollo, once buried beneath tons of volcanic rock, now appears fully intact, his bronze knee shining in the sun, body lunging forward into action, ready to move.

And, of course, there are the bodies. The citizens killed by the volcanic eruption were encased in layers of pumice and ash, sealed for centuries within the wreckage. As the ash rained down, some residents tried to crawl to safety, arms attempting to drag bodies out. Others curled into themselves or lay down to rest. And some reached for one another, heads leaning against chests, arms wrapped around arms, bodies intertwined. The eruption swallowed them whole. As these corpses decayed, they left behind a void in the shape of themselves. Upon excavation, researchers poured plaster into these absences, what had effectively become molds of the living as they became dead, and they rediscovered the shape of loss.

Sabino Canyon, where I sometimes run, is partially shaped by water. It's a dozen miles north of where I live, and rain consistently collects there. The canyon was initially formed as an absence, the necessary dip beneath mountains, but the bowl has been cut deeper by water. Stretching out in the shadow of the Catalinas, the area averages twelve inches of rain annually, more than most desert biomes, and in the summer, the monsoons slip down the basin's slopes, leaving tear tracts, water sinking into shallow roots and carrying sediment past squat shrubs and tall saguaros and into the creek, where—unless the stream froths over fallen boulders or snags on big branches—it flows like glass, clear and uninterrupted. These rains sand down the bowl of the canyon, moving dirt and rocks further downstream, emptying open the creek's starting point.

These rains, like all rains, come from an overflow changing form. After evaporating from the land, from rivers or puddles or sodden soil, water vapor hangs in the sky. I can't see it, but I can feel it. It's the heaviness in the air, the wetness that weighs on me when I clamber up dusty trails. This part of the water system is invisible, but it wraps around me, like love or fear or some other haunting the eye can't see. As these water molecules release energy, rising up and slowing down, they huddle together, condensing into droplets that constellate into clouds. These droplets appear to be floating, but they are, in truth, falling slowly, so slowly the eye can't track their movement. The wafts of cirrus and ribbed altocumulus and towering cumulonimbus clouds, they all, over time, sink into the basin's red bowl. As they fall, some of the cloud's droplets touch other droplets and coalesce, joining hands, protons. As the droplets gather mass, they gather speed, connecting with more drops, and gaining more weight, and falling faster, and connecting with more drops, and gaining more weight, and falling faster, and so on and so on. When the weight of water becomes too much, the swollen droplet overflows the cloud and rains down between the canyon's walls, unrecognizable as its old self and, at the same time, chemically unchanged. I'm trying explain that Sabino Creek is the sky come down.

One morning in early summer, I drove out from the center of the city and paid five dollars to park on hot asphalt and run the canyon's hilly trail. The paved road curves into the basin, and the path crosses the creek nine times on bone-colored stone bridges. The first monsoon of the season had ravaged the city the night before, soaking the roads and tamping down the dirt. The creek was high, so high it ran over and under Sabino's bridges, small gullies swirling around their retaining walls. At the first bridge, the lowest one, I slipped off my shoes, stuffed my socks inside, and picked them up by their tongues. My feet glowed white; it looked as if they'd never seen the sun. I watched them tiptoe to the edge of water like they were someone else's feet. I took one step at a time, bracing myself against the cold shock of water. It almost hurt, how refreshing it was. The water magnified my feet, and as the sun glinted off the sloshing current, I remembered Noah shepherding his animals to safety and the way the water rose around them. I remembered my hometown's flood and the broken roads and homes and bodies. I remembered laying Dad to rest. The dark waves and the hot, heavy air. The smell of plough mud lingering.

At the bridge's center, the water deepened, but I didn't realize it until I'd planted my leg in the current and soaked the edge of my capris. The water crept up like a flood climbing wallpaper. It was a ruin in reverse, taking up more room than was given. I felt the fabric of my leggings go soggy, absorbing all that it could hold, and I realized I was stranded. There was no going back. For a moment, I just stood at the center of the bridge in high water. The saguaros bathed in the sun, the shrubs lazed along the trail, and the canyon walls ran steep around me. The world smelled of creosote and sweat. Cactus wrens sputtered their song like a car that wouldn't start. A gush of current slapped my leg, water meeting body, and like an animal that had survived when all its kin died, I bolted. Relying on some instinct shelved inside me, I pivoted my back leg forward and pranced to the other side, someone else's stark white feet flashing through the fallen sky.

CHILDHOOD EULOGY

*Y*ou were a boxy car and "Dad, what does this lever do?" I was young, not even in grade school, my legs so short my feet couldn't touch the mat; they just swung above it. You were the small hitch beneath the window, pulled before an answer. You were the open car door, air rushing in, because I needed to know how everything worked, because I needed to know what I could control and what I couldn't. You were Dad, pulling over, shutting the door and asking me to trust him. I trusted him.

You were the Ramones CD playing on the living room stereo. A rough voice and simple chords. You were not necessarily the lyrics but their cadence, the way you begged for people to hop around in socks on wooden floors, the joy and ridiculous movement of dance, the jumps of "Nothing to do, nowhere to go-oh," the way Dad and I sang with breathy, British accents, "I wanna be sedated."

You were two pigtails and sometimes a French braid. Mostly you were a ponytail because it was easiest to run around with hair out of the way. This was important: the freedom of the body. So, of course, you were not bows.

The dogwood trees blooming, neighbors waving from their porches, the sun gone but the air still warm: you were walks around the neighborhood in the early evening with Dad. You were ice cream at the end of the walk. I always thought of this as a secret, as a time just for Dad and me, safe from the rest of the world, and for a while, it was.

You were the sprinkler I ran through at the same time as another girl, water like opaque glass, the warmth, the wetness. The sidewalk and the hidden sky and the bathing suit I wore. You weren't goggles because I didn't know I needed them, but you were the scrape I got when the other girl fell on top of me. She'd run at the same time as me, entered from the other side of the sprinkler, but I never saw her coming. You were my scar; the way Dad tended the wound, constant with care.

You were never ear infections, and often you were perfect attendance. This was more luck than anything else. You were a lot of math games and worksheets. You were two plus one equals blank and if I have three oranges and give two away, how many do I have? What am I left with?

I mean you were tonsils and adenoids, meaning you were too big to swallow. You were suffocating. At night, when I rasped, startling myself awake with a lack of oxygen, Dad heard me, and he knew how to help. He flashed a flashlight down my throat and saw you glisten.

You were the hospital, the needle, the numbing cream, the screaming. You were high pitched and sharp, a knife splitting almonds.

You were popsicles and pudding. You were reruns of *Matlock*.

You were vanilla yogurt, the kind I ate for breakfast.

––––––––

Eventually, you were just a story to tell friends.

You were the protective goggles my brother and I wore when we chiseled away at fake fossils on the kitchen counter, two siblings eager to find bone, dust coating the Formica like dried sweat on skin. You were the protective goggles Dad insisted I wear even though they were a little too big. "Better safe than sorry," he said.

You were the chickenpox I gave a family friend at our chicken-pox party, the ones that sent him to the hospital but just made me itch. We ran around in the yard, playing tag and letting the grass squish beneath our bare feet. That virus still swims in my body, sure, but it hasn't bitten my skin since. I sometimes wonder: why was I lucky? Back then, when red dots pockmarked my body, you were just a lot of hydrocortisone cream.

You were my bike in the Richland Fashion Mall parking lot, the floor still dark despite the overhead fluorescents, stream-ers rustling in the breeze. Dad pushed me, one hand on the handlebars and one on the seat, steadying me. He ran beside me, and then let go. A classic movie scene, almost too clichéd to be true.

Then, it was just me and you. No one to save us.

You were gravity winning and then you weren't. You were the brakes I still needed to learn how to use. You were badges of honor: scraped elbows. You were pain, overcome.

You were sips from Dad's Diet Coke, sweet aspartame that made me hunger for more.

Did you know what was coming? Did you know that soon the pain would never go away? I want to slow down. Let me have this happiness for just a little while longer, please. Let me stay here, please.

Once, you were Dad's car in my high school parking lot, me behind the wheel. Old Green Day turned low on the radio, then clicked off for concentration. You were the pollen lines curved by rain. You were the pine needles I eased over and the smell of evergreens in the air. You were the brakes, jolting. My hands, sweaty. You were the curbs I hit and then didn't, the white lines I parked over and on and in between. Dad was patient with me. He let me take all the time I needed, meting out minutes like the ticker tape would never end.

You were the conjugation of *être* and photosynthesis and derivatives. You were good grades. A small bus on the way to a math competition. You were numbers. A ribbonned medal emblazoned with a calculator and division symbol.

You were that boy's broken femur, the one he cracked in half during a game of pickup soccer. We drove him to the hospital in Dad's car, Dad in the driver's seat, me in the passenger, and him laid out across the back. You were his low, constant moans. The speed bumps we drove over, slow, the railroad tracks we couldn't avoid. We could only listen as he cried over his broken body.

You were the car, first a silver Volvo, then a silver Mazda. The calculated gas mileage at the gas station, the equations Dad made me run through, the numbers that told us how far we could go with what we had.

You were a growth in Dad's pancreas, a tumor. Mom did not call you cancer, but that's what you were.

You were Sufjan Stevens, "Impossible Soul," the longest track on the album over and over and over again, alone on the drive to school. If I got to the parking lot early enough, before too many other people were milling about, I would sink down in my seat and listen as I watched the sky. The pulp of my body scraped out.

You were diet lemonade because what if the Diet Coke had caused the cancer?

You were big armchairs beside IV drips. Room temperature yellow Gatorade because the cold interfered with the medicine. You were cancelled runs. Swollen ankles. You were one thing, and then, all at once, another.

Dying. You were dying.

I can say that now, now that you've been gone for the better part of a decade. At the time though, I couldn't even think it. Some things were beyond imagination. I thought I would see the end for what it was. I thought I would know, that it wouldn't come until I was ready. Sometimes hope looks like foolishness.

You were WebMD at night. I huddled under a thin sheet in bed with my phone, cocooning myself. You were a 7 percent five-year survival rate, but I didn't tell anyone this because I couldn't say the words. I couldn't speak those numbers, make them real in my mouth.

You were thick envelopes in the mail for my brother, the ones he opened at the dining room table with the whole family huddled around like we were hungry for a feast. You were his fingers, greedy for the insides, an imagined future.

You were expensive college tuition. You were pain killers and the CD Dad handed me, the pen he tried to write on it with. What CD were you? I can't remember now. Does it matter?

You were his slurred words, more slurred than any drunk speech I've ever heard, an electric guitar slide I couldn't track. "Yes, we can sell that," Mom said as she took the disc and told me to go to my room. She knew not to puncture the world he lived in, to let him think that everything would be okay, to let me think the same. And, really, she thought it, too. We thought you would be okay.

You were the yogurt Dad covered himself in, the yogurt he thought was hydrocortisone cream. The invisible bites he thought he had. The pain pills. The pain. You were the wet paper towel Mom cleaned the couch with. The couch.

You were vanilla yogurt, the kind I ate for breakfast.

I remember: you were the blueberry muffins we made while the miracle drug dripped into Dad's IV. You were the blueberries, so ripe, almost purple, a deep bruise. You were the red mixing bowl and the spatula I used to stir the batter. Dad usually stirred, but with his backpack filled with the miracle drug slung over his shoulder, his tubes got in the way. You were the tubes, but you weren't the miracle drug. Nothing was the miracle drug.

You were lime green bracelets that said "It's not about the numbers," except it was about the numbers. Cancer growing; white blood cells depleting. You were the numbers.

You were ice chips slipping down the throat, coughing. You were the corner hospital room, the one we moved to after the first one got too crowded.

You were Dad's car on the drive home that night, the night they told us he would make it through. Mom in the driver's seat, me in the passenger, my throw-up smeared across the silver door.

The slim birch tree I held when Mom pulled over to let me empty the nothingness inside me.

You were time slowed down, molasses, a minute stretched like taffy. You were prayers, even though I wasn't sure it would do anything.

You were his breath, the effort it took to breathe, the air scratching at his esophagus. You were that rasp, the sound that won't leave me.

You were Dad's hand, cold and heavy. The last piece of him I touched.

You weren't my eighteenth birthday or my twentieth or my twenty-first. What did numbers matter after? You weren't half a can of Bud Light on prom night. You weren't a bottle of gin in a dorm room. The way it felt cold, then warm, and then, nothing felt like anything at all.

You weren't a mysterious illness, one that left me tired, pulled vials of blood from my "good veins" and gave me nothing in return.

You weren't my car, the silver car, Dad's old car, ramming into brick walls, denting the front and back bumper. You weren't the tire swerving, smashing into a raised curb, the way a hole shredded open on impact. At the shop, the mechanic looked at the old tire stowed in my trunk. "Man," he said, "that's really gone."

You weren't majors and minors, picking out colleges. You weren't waist-deep snow, the chill that made my cheeks ache. I couldn't stop smiling. The covered lawn, the library, the clock. You weren't the kitchen counter, the letter, the way Mom and

I sobbed. It was Dad's alma mater, but I turned it down. It was too expensive. You weren't the ache that never left, my life cleaved between what is and what could have been.

Years after you were gone, I read Didion's *Slouching towards Bethlehem*. "It is easy to see the beginnings of things, and harder to see the ends." But I know exactly when you ended. You couldn't exist without Dad. Maybe what Didion means is that it's harder to *look* at the ends of things. Almost ten years later, I still crinkle when I hear the Ramones.

You weren't dance floor make-outs, arms trailing bodies. Waists, thighs, chests, lips. You weren't misplaced hunger. I ate anything I could; I tried desperately not to collapse.

You weren't *Frankenstein* or the epistolary mode. You weren't heavy textbooks that curved my spine, my statistics class, or the years or days. You weren't numbers I could manipulate.

You weren't a crowded music festival with songs that vibrated my bones. All those bodies, sweating, swaying. You weren't Anderson Paak or MUNA or Sylvan Esso. You weren't the Jack and Coke I drank outdoors waiting for the next act, the way the liquid slid down my throat, cool and traceable until it dispersed, until it disappeared.

You weren't Diet Coke.

Why weren't you a different DNA sequence? Why weren't you higher blood cell counts or a shrinking tumor? Why were you take and not give? You were so many things, so why weren't you a miracle?

A SOFT-BOILED EGG HELD IN A SILVER CUP

or centuries, it was considered taboo, unethical, and morally corrupt to dissect cadavers, and so until the third century BCE, it wasn't done; but in Alexandria, under powerful patrons that pushed for innovation, in a place where Aristotle's separation of soul from body was espoused, a place that wanted to become a scientific and artistic center of civilization, Herophilus of Chalcedon took sharpened metal and placed it against human skin—that symbol of wholeness, oneness, cohesion and completion, that epidermic limit that wasn't to be transgressed—and he pushed the body open.

For several decades, he and his younger contemporary, Erasistratus of Ceos, performed systematic dissections of cadavers. Known respectively as the father of anatomy and the father of physiology, the two physicians studied the ventricles of the brain, described seven pairs of cranial nerves, marked nerve trunks as motor or sensory, distinguished layers in the eye (the cornea, retina, and choroid coat), discovered the heart valves and their functions, and detailed descriptions of the liver, genitals, and pancreas. With this sudden growth of knowledge, there was an urgent need to disseminate the newfound information to other physicians, to help other practitioners help other patients, to share the truths they found, so art and science collided in medical textbooks to expose the body. What words couldn't show, images detailed. It was the first time medical illustrations were used for instruction, and it seemed as if the body would be unlocked, its inner workings laid bare on sheets of papyrus. But Herophilus and Erasistratus died, Alexandria burned, and dissection was made illegal once again. The merging of art and science in medical illustrations stalled for several hundred more years, sliced clean from history, and the body stayed shut.

The figure begins at the waist, skin flipping up on itself like pants half-pulled inside out. The red edge of the torso gives way to a pale stomach, skin marbled through with dirty green. The surface of the body looks dull and cold, a fever-stricken Victorian. There's only one arm, the left, held aloft and crooked so the broken elbow points skyward. The head folds back into this crook, or where the head should be folds back. The fact is none of Berlinde De Bruyckere's sculptures have heads. In the early nineties, she began exhibiting work, using blankets to gesture toward the absence of the body, and over the years, she moved closer to the human frame, eventually molding its skin and innards into familiar shapes. Now, sculpture after sculpture of cold wax depicts contorted bodies, but still, there are never heads. "The figure as a whole," she says of her *Suture* exhibit, "can express a mental state making the presence or absence of a head irrelevant." The body, she means, is always speaking.

Looking at this sculpture, this life-size torso housed in a glass box and hung from a wall, this piece called *The Muffled Cry of Unrealizable Desire*, I saw myself. Tomorrow would be the fourth anniversary of my dad's death, and I was in Vienna, in the Leopold Museum, alone with these torn bodies. The walls were big, white, mostly empty, and I was dwarfed, wrapped in the space. I spent hours wandering the *Suture* exhibit, circling sculptures and drifting between them. I felt the open air push in on me. To others, I must have looked lost, in a daze, and perhaps I was.

It was the loneliest time in my life, and for the first time, I saw it. Desire fell free from its object in that wax, and I saw what I'd become: irrevocably lonely. I'd moved hundreds of miles away from my family, the only people who could understand my grief, a misguided attempt to outrun pain, and while people were still around me, friends even, they couldn't touch what pulsed inside me. Instead of mapping the pain within, opening my chest's cabinet and letting the body's geography breathe, I shut my loss up inside myself and closed down all roads leading in.

Two years before I visited Vienna, two years after Dad died, I went to the doctor to try to find the root of my fatigue, a mystery that would never be sufficiently solved. I was in college and would come back to my dorm room after class to lie in bed. I felt exhausted listening to lectures on eighteenth-century English literature, walking the brick pathways between back-to-back classes, flipping handwritten pages in the library to study for exams. After each small task, a shower, a workout, a walk to buy coffee, I needed to do nothing for an hour, to let my body recover and prepare to move again. In this way, I lost mornings, afternoons, days to the abyss.

I'd just entered my twenties, and I should've had more energy than ever. I hoped this lack would go away on its own, so I waited weeks, then months, scribbling notes in class, scooping bland pasta into cafeteria bowls, lying on the quad's soft grass with friends, but the fatigue yawned on. Eventually, I couldn't remember when the tiredness began. Mom told me to go to campus health. "It could be your thyroid or your iron," she said, "an easy fix."

The nurse weighed my barefoot body on a hallway scale, squeezed a blood pressure cuff tight across my bicep, and handed me a two-item checklist on a half sheet of paper to determine if I was depressed. When she stuck a needle in my arm, I looked away. I disliked watching the sharp point puncture skin, didn't like to see the moment when the self broke open; it was a violence I had a hard time making myself watch, that cleaving. Metal pushing against tense skin, the elasticity and surrender. De Bruyckere said, "The skin is the container of the soul," and back then, I worried that, if punctured, my body might leak all over everything, that the wreckage could be terrible and irreversible, a flood you can't rewind. Years later, I'd learn that this was common in grief, that the bereaved worried sadness unleashed could blanket everything, but at the time, when the nurse moved her needle toward my skin, I didn't know it, so I turned away, wincing in a private shame.

As the nurse filled five glass vials with my blood, I turned back. Even though I hated the breakage necessary to see my innards, I was entranced by the body turned inside out. My blood was deep red, burgundy, the color of boiled raspberry jam, and I had the urge to reach out and hold the vials, to weigh them in my palms, feel the warmth I could create. In that moment though, in the doctor's office, sitting in a plush chair, I didn't. I just sat there, watching the nurse pull blood from me, watching a part of myself be drained away.

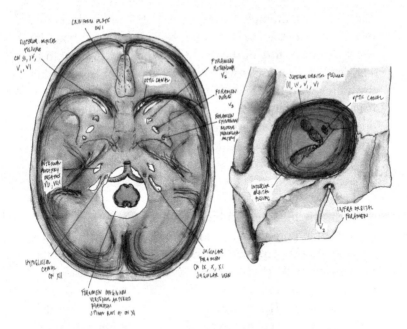

Figure 1. Is it possible to know the body's inner workings without wounds?

In 1506, Leonardo da Vinci watched a one-hundred-year-old man die. He watched the man's lungs tremble, his chest lift, then stay fallen. After the man was declared dead, da Vinci sketched his sleepy face. Then, he took out his scalpel and started dissecting.

Bodies weren't yet preserved, so he had to work quickly, lifting the skin to capture what lay beneath. He detailed the surface muscles, outlining his images in black chalk before over-coating them with ink. As he peeled the skin away, lifting out pieces of the body, he noted the inner muscles and veins, the curvature of the spine, the lungs, the spleen, and liver. He focused on the mechanisms of the body, drawing each muscle and bone from multiple angles, wanting to capture the body's history. Put another way: in cataloguing a cut-open body, he was telling the story of the life that had once lived within it. The dead man's muscles were small, the result of an active life dwindling, and the cleaned bones remained unbroken; he'd been careful around sharp edges. But when da Vinci knifed open the old man's artery, he found it "dry, shrunk and withered." His blood vessels had twisted and been blocked. Some small movement, a turn in sleep, a bend to retrieve a dropped fork, had stopped the flow, created a clot, and the man had died peacefully.

During his lifetime, da Vinci carved open over thirty cadavers, creating more than seven hundred anatomical sketches, studying the skeletal, muscular, nervous, and vascular systems. He understood that the body was a system, that the parts made up the whole, and that to understand its totality, he had to examine its pieces. His illustrations are exquisite, the veins delicate, the muscles deep, and the skull exploded in view. As an artist and engineer, he wanted to know the form and function of the body, where emotions originated and how they traveled. Where did sadness discolor bone? Where did grief burrow down?

These images aren't just about accuracy; they're about beauty, too. The two are related. The hard lines of bones, the bow of muscle, the curls of viscera: you can't separate the aesthetics from the facts. Da Vinci found innards beautiful and tried to sketch them so. He saw thickened veins and marveled at warped arteries, the quick line of blood a swipe on his parchment. He saw the joy in muscles, the pain in viscera, and he bore down on the paper, pushing into the parchment with intensity. In his sketches, the body is filtered through him, through his hand, and maybe that's why he never published them. He could never capture everything; between what he saw and what he rendered, a gulf stretched out.

In the thick of my loneliness, I went out, went to parties, kissed and drank too much. I had fun, but my body felt rote in the actions. I observed myself as an unbiased third party, noting my movements, gestures, the way my body felt. In the middle of a kiss, I would sometimes open my eyes, just to look at the man I was kissing, try to see what he felt that I could not. There was a pane of glass between me and joy. I could see it, I could reach for it, but I couldn't touch it.

I tried to run my body down to understand how it worked. It wasn't intentional, or I wasn't conscious of this intentionality. At night, I threw back shots of cheap vodka, the kind that smelled like gasoline, and fell to my knees on the way to bars and house parties, giddy over the purple bruises sure to form. I danced in dirty basements, the kind college boys brought their own tables to for DJ sets, and at 2 a.m., I'd stumble home, eager for the ache my muscles would feel in the morning. I kissed just to work my lips raw. Every night became the same: a swirl.

In the morning, I poked hickeys in the mirror, inspected my body for damage and smiled when I saw it. I wanted my pain to be exquisite, a jewel I could touch, something I could look at, but the truth was the point of hurt wasn't something I could see. It buried itself in my bloodstream and thyroid, slept in my lungs and unfurled in my knees. I was afraid to touch that true pain, afraid its intensity would kill me, but the touch of anything else paled in comparison. So much felt like nothing. What I saw, this impulsive and indulgent life, was not what I felt. I was floating between here and there, trapped in a void, meaning unreachable, absent, in another dimension. It took years to learn how to pin back my skin, how to gut my own body.

Rope drapes between two wooden trestles, the beams desiccated and rough, and batted cloth sits in the rope's makeshift sling. Carried inside this cradle, climbing out, overflowing, are thick waxen entrails. These intestines curl around each other like insidious or hungry limbs, tangling and untangling, crawling over the cloth, the sawhorses, and each other. Displaced from the body, they reach out for edges, for form and shape, for something to hold them. The gray flesh occasionally sparks red, the innards torquing, writhing. Desperation is made corporeal. It's impossible not to feel, looking at these twisting innards, the way pain and suffering collide with pleasure and beauty.

I remembered how, when I was in first or second grade, my dad broke down our house's deck. The wood was faded and brittle. Splinters were all but guaranteed, and if you were dedicated enough, you could tear off a chunk of wood, pull the deck apart like a pomegranate. It was time for the deck to go. So one day, in early fall, on a day that was citrus crisp, Dad got out his hammer, his crowbar, and a rubber mallet, and he began peeling back the wood. After an hour of hitting, pulling, and swinging, his body was slicked with sweat. It glinted in the sun. I wasn't allowed to help (too dangerous), but I stood behind him and watched. This work enthralled me—how much damage the body could do. Dad brought the mallet over his shoulder, winding up. The sky bore birthmarks of clouds, the wind rustled pecan tree leaves, and I watched Dad's muscles inhale, bellying full, then emptying out as he swung the mallet forward, an inch from my face. I was so close to it, all that pain, all that beauty. He didn't hit me, but he came close. He made me stand inside after that, behind a glass-fronted door.

Years later, I felt the mallet's echo of air as I looked at the sculpture. De Bruyckere's *Inside Me II* isn't housed in a glass box. It sits in the center of a room, the viscera reaching out toward viewers, toward me. The innards are roughly as long as I am tall, so it seems as though the interior of the body outgrew its shell, broke through its cocoon. These entrails grew too big for the skin and had to poke through. There was no other way. But, of course, these entrails aren't just physical innards but internal feelings too; their physicality carries emotional freight. In the sculpture, there's a quiet loss of control, an inability to contain, that frightens me, that calls to me.

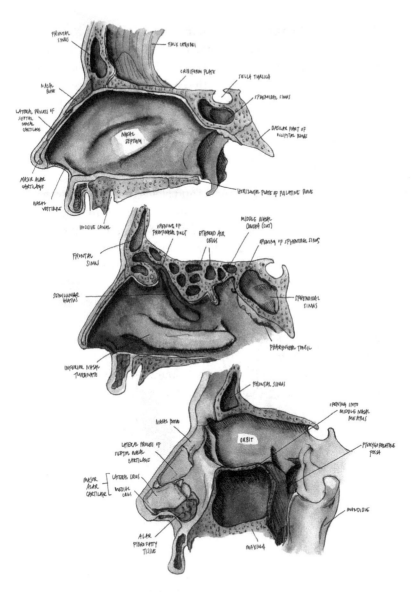

Figure 2. Where is the first incision made?

Two weeks after the doctor took my blood and sent it to a lab, the results came back: nothing. They didn't know what was wrong with me or perhaps they thought nothing was wrong with me. Couldn't they see it in the circles under my eyes, in the puffiness of my cheeks, the way my limbs hung heavy? I was referred to a rheumatologist, one I'd never call. I felt passed off, a burden to be shuttled from one physician to the next. I cried when I saw the results because I knew there was something inside of me that I needed to understand, something that pushed against my internal mechanisms and clogged my moving cogs.

I started looking at medical illustrations, not to diagnose myself, not to discover the root of the problem, but just to feel my own body, understand how it worked. Leafing through Dad's old books, I stopped to admire the images, their edges and curves. My fingers pushed in on my face, squishing down the doughy viscera, and felt for my skull, its open orbits, divots, and ridges. I mapped the hitch of my mandible to my cheek's zygomatic arch, looked for where rigid nasal bone gave way to bendy cartilage, and pressed into the skin looking for the hollow tunnels of my skull's foramen. I knew that I had let the fatigue go on too long, that I had to stop ignoring what my body was telling me. Sometimes I imagined my own autopsy, considered what a doctor would find if they pulled off my skin and sawed open my skull. The body seems discrete from the outside, smooth and simple, but inside it's all overlapping systems, a mess of connections. I looked at the reference book's pictures and saw my own brain, gray matter pinked with blood, its deep grooves slick and sticky, white matter turgid underneath.

The Wound III was inspired by a series of photographs from the nineteenth century. In the archived album, Ottoman women pose after ovarian surgery, their excised tumors sealed beside them in laboratory jars. Like winning farmers at a country fair competition, they stand beside these jars with something akin to solemn pride. *This lived inside me*, they seem to say, and *I survived it.* Some of the women lay a hand on their jar's metal lid, a tender sign of ownership. In the photos, their heads are covered, and their striped dresses crinkle down to their wrists and ankles, but at their bellies, a hole is ripped open in their clothing and a screech of scar peeks through, a second face exposed at the abdomen.

De Bruyckere saw these pictures and they struck her like a guitar player picking a string. Vibrating, she hung leather harnesses on a wall. Inside these harnesses, the same morbid flesh muscled in her other work clings to the fabric's edges, and tattered cloth dangles inside what would be a space. The three materials (leather, flesh, and fabric) sag like a trio of parentheses cupping emptiness. This sculpture asks: can we ever truly isolate pain? Or is it just an opening to everywhere else, to everything else?

I looked at this sculpture from a distance, walking from one side to the other, assessing it from different angles, a pendulum swinging in my dirty Converse sneakers. The leather was dark brown, old, the stitching coming apart. The whole structure hung from a rusted metal hook. I inched closer, then closer, examining the ripe flesh, its tears and slashed scars. The cloth was worn, like a childhood blanket kept too long. There was a sharp intimacy to the work, one that, slowly, I let cut me open.

"The wound is a sign of being," says De Bruyckere in *Suture*, "a hole that makes you aware that the body has an inside. Through the wound, our inner side can be visible to the outside world, which is an essential existential experience. Simone Weil once said, 'Out of the wound the wings can grow.' For me, the wound is a sign of change, a gate to another sphere, to a new life."

A SOFT-BOILED EGG HELD IN A SILVER CUP

At a crowded bar, I stood on the edge of the dancefloor, trying to find my friends. Bodies slid against each other, the air
hot and sticky, the space poorly lit with neon purple lights.
The place was a restaurant during the day, and at night,
workers pushed the dining room tables to the sides. Girls
stood on bench seats, dancing without moving their feet, just
shimmying above the masses. I squeezed lime into my gin
and tonic and watched the spent wedge trundle to the bottom of the glass before sipping the tartness through two coffee straws. I had not yet learned to drink slowly; I knew only
one speed: breakneck. It felt the same as every other night.
It was dark.

A boy walked over and introduced himself. He leaned close,
speaking over the music's pulses, and his breath tickled my ear.
He was visiting my college campus for a singing competition
and went to a university far away, one someone from my high
school attended. I surprised myself and asked if he knew her,
this girl who had known my dad, and miraculously, he did.
They were friends. I felt it, the distance knifed open.

It was 2 a.m., and the lights flickered on. I saw his face
clearly: young, smooth, sweet. I imagined what lay beneath his
skin: his masseter muscle, his zygomaticus major and minor.
I realized that, of course, he could see me clearly too, see the
curves in my orbicularis oculi and the tightness in my risorius,
and for a moment, before my friends found me and swept me
away, before I walked into the cold night and ordered a greasy
hot dog from a late-night food joint, before I collapsed into my
own bed and snored into sleep, this boy and I just stared at
each other, without the darkness between us.

After three to four days, a dead body smelled too much for
anyone to bear. Even before that, you had to be able to with-
stand the stench of decay. And you had to be physically strong,
strong enough to saw open skin, muscle, viscera, and bones. Of

course, you had to be emotionally strong, too. Could you take a knife and slice open skin, not knowing what you'd find?

In 1536, in Padua, the anatomist Andreas Vesalius began dissecting cadavers in earnest, cutting open body after body, sifting through their interiors, reaching inside for understanding. It was the early sixteenth century, and human dissections were not yet sanctioned by the Pope. Cadavers were hard to come by, and Vesalius sometimes resorted to stealing the decaying, discarded bodies of executed criminals. Under the cover of night, he stalked the cobblestone streets, pulling stiff corpses from their resting places, determined to learn what secrets burrowed inside them. Imagine it: the cold turgid skin, the dried blood flaking off, the weight.

After the Pope officially approved human dissection for anatomical studies, Vesalius began performing dissections in packed operating theaters. Students crowded the room. Their breath decorated the space with humidity, and their sweaty handprints adorned the wooden railings. They huddled around the corpse, peering into the body cut open, an open door to another world. The slick sheen of intestines, the gum of fat, the quick puncture of a lung. A community of people were hungry to understand their interiors, even the pieces of themselves that repulsed them. In that room, the skin was peeled away, the ribcage sawed open, and the contents of the body examined, no longer considered unknowable and off-limits.

Vesalius kept constant companionship with his corpses. He recorded his findings as he methodically catalogued the body and its systems, and with this accumulated knowledge, he set out to write a landmark medical text, one founded on findings from cadavers and illustrated with anatomically correct images. It would become one of the most influential texts on human anatomy. He reached back to Alexandria and ripped open the scarring of time. Lost, of course, doesn't mean irretrievable.

He contacted a number of artists and received technically accurate drawings imbued with elegance. The brain cross-sectioned from above, the torso pulled open at the stomach, all the muscles standing without bones. Now, without carving open a cadaver, people could see what swam inside of them. The corpses were posed in lifelike positions, and the body given grace, even in death, perhaps especially so. These cadavers could no longer move, but they could show us the insides of bodies that could. So it was the dead that taught Vesalius about the living, that taught all of us about ourselves. In 1543, he published *De Humani Corporis Fabrica* and created a network of visceral knowledge. He clutched his precious truth: to know the body you had to open it.

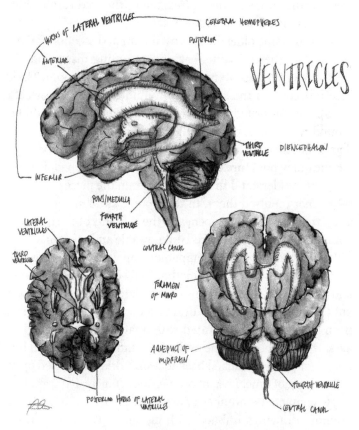

Figure 3. How do you keep wounds open?

She outlines the body in black ink, marking the contours of bones, the meat of muscle, and the edges of skin before filling the image with watercolors. She coats the brain's ventricles in electric blue, paints the falx cerebri sea green, and shadows the optical canal. Her work is accurate, filled with labels and close-ups and cross-sections, but there's a beauty in it that can't be quantified. The ink bleeds into the paint, and the hard edges soften in water, dispersing like a bruise.

I first saw Kristina Alton's work when I was sitting on the edge of a pool in North Carolina. I was visiting a friend, and as we basked in the sun, she pulled out her phone to show me Kristina's images. They were friends, both affiliated with the university where I did my undergrad, the same university two of Dad's medical partners graduated from decades earlier, which as a detail is logically irrelevant but emotionally important.

"I think you'll like her stuff," my friend said as she waded into the water. My feet piddled on the surface of the cold pool, not yet hot enough to take the plunge, and I looked at Kristina's illustration of the brain on my friend's phone. I held the cross-sections in my hand, zooming in and out, careening over the folds like a crop duster outlining the rows of a field. The canals of the ventricles, the overgrown walnut of the cerebellum, the small balloon of the pons: it captivated me. I scrolled through her feed, ravenous for more, and inhaled sharply as I dunked my feet into the chilly water, feeling the bite of it.

On the fourth anniversary of Dad's death, I was alone in a strange city. I made a plan for myself, for the day, thinking *what would Dad want to do?* I was ready to let my innards splay, to let grief knife me open, to let my body touch everything outside myself.

A SOFT-BOILED EGG HELD IN A SILVER CUP

At a small coffee shop–bookstore called Phil, I ordered the full breakfast, and it came on a red cafeteria tray. Two rolls, two types of cheese, three slices of meat, and a soft-boiled egg held in a silver cup. I didn't know how to open the egg, so I had to ask the waitress, who found this vulnerability charming. She ran a line around the brown shell with a knife, then watched me crack it open. I tapped the silver spoon on the head of the egg, heard the soft crunch, and lifted to see warm insides. The yolk was gooey, and I tore off a piece of bread, dipped it in yellow. The food slid down my throat and settled in my stomach. After I finished my latte, I ran my finger down the spines of a dozen books, including *The Manly Art of Knitting*, where, on its front cover, a cowboy sat on a horse, knitting needles in hand. I smiled; Dad would've liked it.

At the butterfly garden, fragile creatures feasted on apple slices and sweet nectar. The greenhouse was humid, sweat beading on the windows, and I understood loneliness to be this humidity, to be hanging everywhere, touching everything, every part of me. I gave myself into the embrace. I felt the tense places in my body, my shoulders and neck, paid attention to the quietness in my legs, and listened for the blood pumping through. Next door to the garden, in the grand library, the one with the marble steps and angelic murals painted on the ceiling, sat a plaster cast of Emperor Franz Joseph's right hand, a piece of his body preserved in art.

After I cooled off from the greenhouse, I walked down side streets and around city squares until the modern art museum rose up before me. Dad would've thought much of the plain abstractness weird, so inside, I took selfies imitating the art. There's a picture of me, sweaty, wide eyed, and staring at the camera, and behind me, an all-black painting. Life imitates art. I looked at Picassos, Mirós, and Giacomettis, paintings and sculptures of the body contorted to reveal emotion, and I ate a frankfurter on the museum steps.

Years earlier, years before Dad died, before he was sick, in Paris, on a hot summer day, we walked the catacombs. It was cool beneath the city, damp, and the skulls and bones were dimly lit. I felt drawn to these bodies whose lives lived on after death, beneath the bustle of people's feet, holding up their lives lived out in the sun. On the fourth anniversary of Dad's death, remembering this, I descended a windowless stairway to the Austrian royal family's crypt. The caskets were big, made of metal whose sheen had dulled, adorned with skulls and crowns and skulls wearing crowns. I allowed myself to feel what I needed to feel: loneliness, sorrow, love, joy. The royal family was both here and not here, caught between the binary of living and dead, their corpses present but their beings gone. There was no way to resolve this contradiction, to recognize that Dad was always with me but he would never be here again, so I sat in the tension, let it tear into my body and saw open my insides. Eventually, I climbed back up to the sun, opened. It felt better, not to be contained.

CARVE US NEW

t begins with absence. It begins over 2,500 years ago, in India, without noses. The written story is a game of telephone: Henri Dutrochet, a French physician, wrote a letter to the editor recounting his brother-in-law's experience as an army officer in India: one of his brother-in-law's subordinates punished one of his own subordinates by cutting off the man's nose: the now-noseless man went to locals (known for their reconstructive surgery) for help: and having peeled back the layers of colonial violence, we arrive at the beginning of the story of skin grafts: absence.

The space where the man's nose had been was already beginning to scar, new skin edging over the wound like tissue paper wrapped around a red sweater. Locals opened the wound to prevent scarring, the thin healing torn off in preparation for a transplant. According to the letter, the patient's ass was "beaten with an old shoe." After being hit into numbness, a triangle of swollen skin was marked and cut, fat clinging to skin, blood slicking it all. The inflamed skin was placed in the old wound, where it attached and grew, self replacing self. Over time, the graft became indistinguishable from uninjured skin, so much so that people may have forgotten the injury existed, even with the invisible evidence centered on the face.

This summer, a few days after the seventh anniversary of my dad's death, a high school friend's dad died. Something in me split open. Aaron was a year ahead of me, but he was friends with my brother, and we had math class together. Usually, he sat a few rows in front of me, and we both wore collared shirts, like everyone else in school. He used to call about calculus, asking me to walk him through an operation as I sat in my living room, and he sat in his room, and we both leaned over sharply penciled numbers. I'd explain a derivative, he'd follow along, and we'd move over our respective pages like airplanes looking down on fields, but really, he didn't call for homework help. Really, he called to talk. We were consecutive valedictorians. At our Episcopal school's graduations, we read from the Bible in front of fifty classmates and their families in a big, drafty church. My dad watched Aaron take the podium. He didn't watch me. Seven summers after my dad died, his did.

I'd been home most of that summer, the summer his dad died, and happy, miraculously. The year before was hard; I lost friends who told me my grieving was a burden, who told me missing my dad made them uncomfortable, who said I cried too much. They couldn't live with loss, and I couldn't live without it. I'd flown home in May, left the desert for humid South Carolina, red-brown dirt for overgrown green, and I spent my days reading and writing and watching comfort TV with my mom and her dog. I felt loved, I laughed easily, my face turned up, and then, Aaron's dad died, and I felt the thin membrane of time rip.

My feet tingled in their plastic booties. For thirty minutes, I sat on a half-empty blue-jean loveseat with my feet taped in plastic and coated in minty liquid. My mom sat on another couch, perpendicular to me, her feet taped into her own booties, the dog curled up beside her. The lights were off in the living room, and outside, a storm broke through clear skies. Onyx Peeling Callus-Removing Booties come in red and white packs of two and claim to accelerate the sloughing off of dead skin. They help peel back epidermal layers to expose greater tenderness. All summer, Mom and I had walked barefoot over hot ground: we hip-hopped on asphalt to take the dog to the bathroom, we tiptoed over concrete to jump into the pool, and we ran over sand to soak in the sea. With every step, time had accumulated on our callused feet, each layer of hardness added for protection, but at some point, it was too much. I could cradle my heel and feel nothing.

At the local grocery store, we decided it was time to soak away our hardness, to shrug off some of the dead skin. Veering down the beauty aisle, we grabbed two pairs of booties and dropped them in our cart. My grandmother, Mom's mom, was in the hospital, lungs at 60 percent capacity, and we knew it was the top of the descent. At the house, we cut the booties open at their ankles, secured them on our feet with red-tinted tape, and waited. Our plastic socks crinkled as we watched the end of a murder mystery on TV. After thirty minutes, we removed the booties, washed our slick feet in the bathtub basin, and waited for our bodies to unravel.

In 1817, another skin graft was performed, a thumb smeared with disease, a body in need of division, a hurt healed and swaddled in stories. At sixteen, Sir Astley Cooper moved to London to study surgery, though his interest was minimal, until one day his teacher, tired of his pupil's laziness, sawed the arm off a corpse, took it home where Astley lodged with him, and dropped it in front of his student. The boy looked up. The skin was pale, the blood still, muscles stiff and spilling out. The arm smelled rank as decomposition took hold. The teacher told Astley, "Dissect it."

After that, Sir Astley considered every day without dissection a failure. He felt drawn to this surgical work, pulled to expose the interior of the body in order to heal the whole of it. Day after day, he watched the glint of a scalpel push through skin and into blood. The metallic smell never left him. He was brutal, taking on jobs others wouldn't, gruesome surgeries, because he knew that inflicting temporary pain was sometimes the most compassionate thing to do. Four years into Cooper's tenure as anatomy professor at the Royal College of Surgeons, an unnamed observer recorded in the surgeon's notebook an account of a graft onto an amputated thumb:

> 1st week to July 25th, union seems to have taken place.
>
> 2nd week to August 1st, Mr. Cooper proved the vascularity of the newly attached portion by pricking it very slightly with a point of a lancet, which produced fluid blood as readily as from any other part of the joint. Sensibility has not returned.
>
> 3rd week from operation. In the course of this week sensation has returned in the end of the stump.

A field of skin was pulled up and placed in a sea of blood. It attached. When pierced, it bled. When pricked, it hurt. The graft was declared a success when the skin could feel again, when pain came back to it.

Loss both repelled and attracted me. Others' wounds made me scratch at my own scabs, curdled skin caught beneath prying fingernails, a painful reopening I wanted to avoid, especially this summer, when I'd been happy for the first time in a year, when I went to the movies again and made skillet-burst tomato pasta and read books about women pioneers in STEM fields. But I also knew that a wet wound, an open wound, was best for healing.

In college, I became friends with a girl the year after her dad died. In graduate school, I bonded with someone whose dad died a few years before mine. We could talk about our fathers in ways we couldn't with anyone else. We could talk about loss as a part of our lives. "That was my dad's favorite ice cream flavor." "He was the one that taught me about birds." "We used to love swimming together." There's an undeniable attraction between those whose parents die early. We find each other without effort, pulled into one another by the emptiness within us.

It happens almost immediately: when my dad died, Caitlin, a childhood friend, was there for me. She was there when Dad was diagnosed, and she was there when he went into the hospital, and she was there when he didn't come out. "Welcome to the club," she said as she hugged me. Our bones dug into each other's bodies. She was taller than me, and I buried my head in her shoulder. Her sweatshirt smelled of laundry detergent and hair product. She held me steady as I wept; to this day, she holds me steady. Her mom died when we were in third grade from the same cancer that killed my dad. If loss subtracted from a person, we'd be slivers of waning humans, waiting for the next death to carve us new.

On the third day, my foot started to peel. Or, rather, I started to peel it. It looked like fake snow had been sprinkled on my soles. The skin was shearing along the halo of my heel, flakes of myself attempting to stay with me, but I didn't want to wait for it to fall off on its own. The chemical peel disrupted the connections between dead skin, and these isolated cells were beginning to slough off. On the blue-jean loveseat, I pried the dead skin from the living, one paper-thin peel the size of my thumb. I barely felt it, just long, thin pressure along the underside of my foot. The inside of the peeled skin was rough, lines raised to fill in the corresponding ridges underfoot. Held up to the light, rivulets of me patterned the world. I showed the sloughed skin to Mom. "Nothing!" she said, "Those things did nothing for me." She raised her calloused heel in evidence.

We were at the beach, and we thought the grains of sand might exfoliate our skin, help shed more dead cells from the soles of our feet to open them to tenderness, to the touch of others and to the touch of self, so we pulled baseball hats onto our heads and walked the dog along the shore where we scattered Dad's ashes. We didn't talk about much. My grandmother was getting a biopsy and was a month away from being diagnosed with dementia. Gulls circled above us as the wind curled off the water and cooled our faces. We ground our feet into the sand and didn't notice volunteers running out of the dunes. They flagged us down and, as they caught their breath, cautioned us to stay away from the marked areas; birds were nesting there.

Wooden posts were pushed into the sand with bright orange caution tape cordoning off sections of the beach. The laminated bulletins stapled to these posts noted that shore birds were laying eggs in the area, but they didn't mention which birds specifically, or who was protecting them from what, only that generations of avian families were seeking refuge here.

In the beginning, no one recorded their own grafting work. It was someone outside who found the work remarkable, who thought the healing a small miracle and wrote down the act. Perhaps it's the dailiness of the doctor-patient relationship that kept physicians from thinking their work miraculous: it's an everyday familiarity, an ordinary intimacy that feels medically commonplace. Doctors talk to patients and heal their bodies; it's all in a day's work. Still, there's an inherent closeness in taking the patient's skin and moving it over blood, in pruning and replanting cells. There's a magic between patient and doctor that those outside might not be able to touch, but they can see it, and they can want it.

In 1818, three Dutch students visited Bünger, a German physician. One of the students wrote about the visit in his diary. Maybe he thought that by recounting the experience, putting it in his own script, he could preserve the hurt and healing. Maybe he knew that the body is the best storyteller, and he wanted to translate its tale into text. Maybe he was attempting to recapitulate the intimacy of corporeal language for others. Whatever his motivations, the graft was kept pressed in those pages until three years later, when Bünger, only at the invitation of a medical journal, published his own report.

Using the letter from India as a guide, the physician beat a woman's upper thigh with a leather belt, cut a strip of inflamed skin with half the fat still attached, and placed the wet segment where a nose had been, sewing the self into place. In his article for *Journal der Chirurgie und Augen-Heilkunde*, Bünger wrote, "We doctors looked at each other in silence and did not believe our eyes when we saw that a graft which the day before had been chalk-white and had been deprived of the vital forces from the remainder of the body for at least 90 minutes, now had become a nose."

In the words of my brother, Aaron had "a massive crush" on me in high school. At the time, I knew this but chose to ignore the facts. The way he texted to confirm assignments, the way he laughed longer at my jokes, the way his eyes flickered away when I turned to face him—I let it all slide past me. It wasn't hard. My junior year, Dad was diagnosed. Before the start of my senior year, he was dead. In between, this:

A warm night supervising a children's campout at school. Tents staked into soft grass, night humming with katydids. The third and fourth graders were zipped into their tents, most of their chatter dropped to whispers, then snores. Aaron and I sat on the cold concrete beneath the cubist-inspired math and science building. He made some joke, said something offhand about hating me, I don't remember what, but I remember this—how everything stopped when he looked at me, how the children were quiet, how the night wasn't buzzing, when he turned to me and said, "I don't hate you, *at all*. You know that, right?" He held my face in his eyes, steady. It was dark and the other high school supervisors were watching a movie inside. The air stood still. I started drawing shapes on the concrete, the ridges of the cement vibrating against my finger, but he kept looking at me. There was surety in his stillness. It was a truth stripped of concealment. A pure attempt at connection. I laughed or shrugged or smirked. I don't know what I did; I don't remember. But I know I broke the moment because he looked inside me and saw what I was trying to hide, and for a single second, I felt seen. And then I felt scared.

And yet, despite this fear or perhaps because of it, I will hold this memory close for years, a worry stone kept in my pocket. I'll run my fingers over it to feel the smoothness of it, the purity. This moment is a balm to my anxiety, my worry that no one will ever understand me, because he did. He does. Loss doesn't necessitate isolation. And even though that scares me, it calms me too.

The peeling started naturally between my toes, dead skin bubbling, pulling like webbing, an outer casing growing away. I prodded it on the couch when I was alone, Mom at the office or in another room on the phone with her mom, the dog lying beside me, uninterested in anything I did unless it involved petting her. Sometimes I picked at the skin, peeling away pieces, feeling nothing, resisting the desire to peel until it hurt. I imagined cutting through the dead layer starting at my ankle, pinching the skin off like a sock, letting the ghost foot stand beside my own live one. Or rather fold beside, the skin too soft, too thin to stand alone.

I remembered a demonstration from a college social psychology class. The professor was tall and slender, a mix of Michael Phelps and Novak Djokovic, one of the more attractive instructors at the university. I had a friend in the class who would sometimes bend over her built-in desk to say, "He's so hot," and I'd nod, keep taking notes. It wasn't that I disagreed, but that desire felt far away from me. There was only one thing I wanted, and it blotted out everything else.

One day, the professor called a volunteer to the front of the lecture hall. I forget what lesson he was demonstrating, but he leaned against the desk, legs crossed with leather shoes peeking from beneath his jeans as an eager student from the front half of the classroom scampered to the stage. Sunlight thrummed through the lecture hall's big, clean windows, and outside the wide lawn was speckled with students. At the front of the cream-colored room, the professor told the volunteer to work up some saliva, then swallow, and the student nodded as he gulped. The teacher then reached behind his back, torquing his torso, his polo creasing, before turning back with an empty red Solo cup. "Now, spit in this cup," he told the volunteer, "Drink it." Imagine holding that thin plastic in your hands. Look down at the lukewarm, phlegmy spit. Swallow.

The student grimaced.

But wasn't it the same as swallowing the spit that hadn't left the mouth? Are we not ourselves once we've been dislocated? Even in front of a classroom full of revolted peers, I think I would've swallowed. I never feared the revolting, the spit, the phlegm; I only feared separation, loss. These days, I want to know who else would've swallowed, who else is fractured from their former self, who else would do anything to remember the taste of wholeness. I want to find them and hold them close. I want a classroom full of us, each holding a red Solo cup of spit, each drinking ourselves down, piecing our bodies back together, unashamed.

On one arm, the soft scratch of cotton; on the other, nothing. On one arm, muggy night air; on the other, nothing. On one arm, a warm hand; the other, nothing. In 1824, the German surgeon Johann Friedrich Dieffenbach detailed his treatment of a woman who had lost feeling in half of her body. At the time, the prescription for an unfeeling body was to irritate it. Dieffenbach decided to try an experimental treatment on the woman, reasoning that touching the unfeeling half of the body would be more effective if a feeling piece of skin was planted there and then stimulated. The doctor wanted to see whether skin that had been stimulated, rubbed, made more alive could survive surrounded by a plane of skin more dead. He wanted to see if deadened skin could be awakened by more vital surroundings.

After rubbing the inside of the patient's elbow with alcohol, holding the arm with a firm tenderness while he swabbed the crook back and forth, he cut a coin-size piece of skin and exchanged it with untouched skin cut from the back of the elbow. Each piece was placed in new wounds, moved front to back, back to front. Six days later, the skin that hadn't been rubbed remained unattached, floating in pus. The stimulated skin, though half decayed, was half alive, attached. The rubbed skin retained the memory of touch and sustained itself until it was accidentally ripped away when the dressing was changed. This newly opened wound bled. The blood was a symptom of life returned.

At the tail end of summer, I left Mom and flew back to Arizona, where I was teaching and studying. I was nervous about coming back to a place I'd left crying, a place that held no piece of Dad, except, of course, for me. As classes loomed, I tidied my adobe casita and found one of Dad's teaching awards, a wooden plaque with black overlay engraved with his name. Notes from some of his hyperbaric oxygen lectures huddled below it, the printed slides annotated with his own small and neat writing. I imagined sitting in the class when he taught. I'd choose a seat near the back, so that I could see the whole room, the sparse and then clumped groups of people there to listen to my dad. The group of button-downs near the front, shaking hands and talking loudly, the polos and dresses murmuring on one side, the suits stiff and quiet on the other. The lecture hall seats themselves would have scratchy fabric, and pink marks of irritation would screech up my legs, but I'd forget them when Dad came in wearing a fox hat, the tail full and plush. After fiddling with the computer and booting up the breathy projector, he'd step in front of the desk and say, "When they told me the name of the lecture hall, I said, 'Wear the fox hat?'" (If you don't get it, say it out loud.)

When he thought he was funny, his whole face rearranged itself, smile wide, teeth crooked, dimples tucked in, and eyes squinting. Before I left for the desert, Mom pointed out that I make this face, too. It was his face I saw when I said something funny, but I hadn't realized I'd absorbed his features into my own, hadn't realize the way my smile parenthesized itself, the way my cheeks rose rounded, the way my eyes squinted into two small tears. When I smiled like this, I doubled. I was both myself and my dad. My smile was his smile, and it brought us back together.

At the end of one week, I wondered if my feet would ever stop peeling, if I would keep collecting balls of dead skin every time I took my shoes off ad infinitum, if each foot would whittle down to the bare minimum: muscle, bones, and sinew contained in a thin bag of dermis. Or maybe my skin would keep growing and shedding, which is what it normally did, but the acceleration of the foot mask made the process visible, made what was continual feel discrete.

As my feet fell apart, my grandmother moved in with my aunt and uncle. My aunt quit her job to take care of her. My grandmother, her memory a swirl, accused my aunt of trying to get her to bathe more than once a day. "You haven't bathed in a week," my aunt said. My grandmother was on oxygen, though she often unhooked the cannula from her nostrils. Her hair, once cut to curl beneath her ears, trellised her shoulders. She stood alone, naked, in front of open windows. How do you care for someone who won't be held?

Mom sent money often and called when she had the courage, but she'd taken care of her mother growing up, and she couldn't do it again. The harder truth to admit, the one that hurt to speak aloud, was that she couldn't watch another loved one die. She worried this made her a bad person, knowing the limits of care, the edges of herself. And yet wasn't she still there for her mom in the ways that she could be? I didn't know how to show her this, how to hold up a mirror so she could see herself. Mom was still watching her die; she was still holding her hand.

The day I left South Carolina, Mom's feet were still hard, the outer skin protecting the tender layers beneath. As I snaked through the airport security line, she walked with me and kissed me on the forehead when she couldn't go any further. I walked through the body scanner, let the machinery peer into my hidden insides, and as I walked out and collected my things, Mom waved from the other side, waiting for me to leave.

The skin on the forearm peeled away from the muscle, shucked off like a cornhusk, an unnamed accident splitting dermis from fat. Though many skin grafts had been performed before, it's this injury, ultimately, that's pinpointed as the true beginning of the procedure. The surgeon Jaques-Louis Reverdin experimentally performed a new kind of skin graft on a thirty-five-year-old male in 1869, planting islands of skin in the open wound instead of more fully filling the absence.

By the time the patient sought treatment, the wound floor had granulated, the open-mouthed injury becoming pink, red, and bumpy, the flesh of wet grapefruit inlaid in skin. The juicy blood vessels looked unnatural exposed to air, a hunger licking the outside world, but in truth, granulation is a sign of healing. No one in this era completed skin grafts on fresh wounds; granulated tissue was thought a necessary prerequisite for a successful graft. Time between hurt and healing was essential.

Reverdin selected the donor site carefully. At the time, some doctors thought these sites could become openings for new diseases, doors to pain that wouldn't shut, but what options did the patients have? To cut skin open was dangerous, but it was necessary for survival, too. The inner arm, flush below the armpit, was often chosen as a donor site because it was smooth and hairless. Hair was considered a problem for grafts because if the follicles stuck too tightly to the bandage, the graft could be ripped away when redressing the wound. The upper thigh was another common donor site (again, hairless), but Reverdin chose the skin from the shin, shaving the man's leg first. Think of the intimacy: kneeling before the patient, smoothing shaving cream over the covered tibia, letting it soften the hair and skin before pulling a wet razor down the leg, careful not to nick the body.

After shaving the man's leg, Reverdin pinched his skin and flicked off a small, thin square. No anesthesia was used when cutting open the donor site. Local anesthetic had yet to be discovered, and complications with general anesthesia heightened the risk of mortality. Numbness was created through beating the donor site, hitting the skin into nonfeeling. Many patients refused grafts because they were afraid of the pain of excision, but what choice did they have?

These small dots of skin were placed in the old wound, where they took hold, reached for one another, formed islands, and, finally, pulled themselves against the edges. As the skin grew, the wound buckled, puckering to contract, distorting the tissue in the process, healing in the form of a scar.

Aaron and I texted daily after his father's funeral. The church had been packed, hot from all those bodies, and my brother and I couldn't wade through them to find Aaron. Because we didn't go to the cemetery for the private burial, we didn't get to talk to him in person. Still, I wanted him to know I had been there, that I saw him, that I understood how the word "dead" stuck like peanut butter in the throat. When we texted, we mostly talked about our lives, where we were living, what we were studying. He wanted to move to Canada; I wanted to go back to the South. He lived in Philadelphia; I lived in Tucson. He was applying for med school; I was almost done with my master's in fine arts. The texts were spurts of questions and winding answers. I wondered, sometimes, if he thought back to that moment with the katydids and the sleeping children and the blue night. I wondered if he held that memory close, if he kept it in his pocket and ran a thumb around it when he felt alone.

We kept texting for months, but with less frequency. Our lives crowded back in, tidal pools filling in as the summer peeled away. We texted during the presidential debates and about the VMAs, about black men and white women and the ways our lives were still being formed. I saw his name on my phone when I walked a desert path at night, when I drank coffee in bed, when I ushered students out of classrooms. Maybe he thought of me when he drove past the only bookstore in our hometown, or when he flew back North, his funeral suit zipped tight in its bag. He didn't tell me what he was looking at when he got the call: the TV, the sidewalk, a tiled bathroom wall. I didn't tell him I wore the same dress to his dad's funeral that I'd worn to my dad's; I've never washed it. We didn't say a lot of things because the truth is what we talked about didn't matter. Underneath the constant communication were two small cuts of skin, reaching for each other.

TAKE MY HAND

om's ring opened. A post in the back connected three silver bands, the center one thin and grooved, the outer two with hands cauterized on them. Each hand was on a different band that was linked by a small pivot so the rings hinged open like a fan. You could pull the hands apart and make them meet again, though when the ring was on your finger, there could be no movement. The hands stayed held. In college, the ring encircled my finger, the hands clasped until one night, after a party, I walked a drunk friend home. He couldn't walk in a straight line, so I let him put his arm around me as we crossed a busy street. "I think you're cool," he said "like, really cool." He was not very good at flirting. When we got to his dorm, he asked me to look away as he threw up in the bushes. The next morning, I noticed one of the ring's hands had been bent and struck off.

I've always had clammy hands. At my middle school graduation, the last graduation of mine Dad saw, the guidance counselor reached out to shake my hand and, on contact, recoiled.

"Are you okay?" he asked. My hands have always been cold, so cold I sometimes wear gloves in the house, and the sweat: that never goes away either. I tell people it's a combination of poor circulation and an athletic lifestyle, which is true, but more truthfully it's my body repelling touch. I don't like to be held. For years, I haven't understood the impulse to hold someone's hand, though I wish I did.

At a party, I see a friend kiss her ex in the kitchen. She raises up on her tiptoes and then lowers back down, her calves bellowing like curtains blown out and in by the wind. In the living room, I ask the person beside me what she thinks of hand holding. "Oh, I love it," she says. "Why?" I ask. The person across from her interrupts me; she loves it, too. The whole table loves it, the whole room, the whole party. They all love it, but no one will tell me why. Granted, this is perhaps not a fun party topic, but it's one I genuinely cannot wrap my head around. When I ask people to explain the compulsion to reach for one another, they flounder, unable to place the automatic into words. Beside me, a man who has been partnered for thirteen years tells me it's just natural, comfortable. He looks off into space as he talks, his cheeks glowing pink, his hands twisting, cutting an indiscernible shape in the air.

A memory from high school: in the car, in the backseat, with the radio low, on the way to a varsity football game. I was in ninth grade, tenth maybe. I looked out the window at the blue night, the way it fell over tilled fields, the dirt shadowed silver by the moon, and when I looked back ahead, my parents were holding hands over the console. The outline of their hands was tinted red and orange by the dashboard, and the heat was blasting on and around but not through their fingers. They were quiet as a golden oldie from 106.7 played in the background, something by the Eagles, I think. They kept their eyes on the road, watching the way it wound toward the school's gates, and yet without looking, without speaking, they found each other.

Our first date was in May of '85. It was his junior year of medical school. It was graduation, and you know I was a house mother at a sorority, because that's how I had room and board and a small stipend. He had asked me out, but there was a function that we had to go to for the sorority because I was the house mother. It was some sort of graduation function—it was informal, it was outdoors. We went to that first, and then we went to dinner and a movie, but dinner was—you already know this part—Caravan, the home of the humpburger, which was a roast beef sandwich. Then we went to see a Coen brothers movie, Blood Simple. *And I still went out with him after that, even though I thought the movie was one of the weirdest things I'd ever seen.*

Fede rings, rings where two hands are cast clasped in metal (like my mother's ring) became popular in the Middle Ages, but they date back to the Greco-Roman period. Some were simple, two gold hands locked together with a personal inscription inside the band, but as time went on, they grew elaborate, the hands slinking from ruffled cuffs, bright enamel coloring wings, stones studding the sides. Though originally given as wedding or engagement rings, over the years, they also became symbols of affection for friends. The name "fede" is extracted from *mani in fede*, Italian for "hands held in faith." Faith as in faith in God, friendship, love.

Five Thanksgivings after Dad died, Mom sliced off the tip of her finger. I was making potatoes au gratin to take over to family friends, and she offered to mandolin the potatoes. Her hands on their dewed bodies, the peeled spuds firm as she ground them against sharp metal, although, maybe not so firm. Her finger slipped or she looked away or she went too far too quickly. Her finger wouldn't stop bleeding—bright red, not dark. The pace kept the color vibrant. It was blood, blood, blood. More blood than I'd ever seen, more than nosebleeds, scrapes, and stitches. She held her hand up, forcing her veins to work against gravity as she pushed a paper towel against the wound. It soaked through. It soaked through again. Dad was dead, so we had to call another doctor, but Mom didn't want us to. "I'm fine," she said, "it'll stop on its own." I gave my brother a look, and he went into another room to dial the number. A physician family friend came over to cauterize the wound, and I saw the pink triangle tip sitting in a pile of sliced potatoes. How many times did she touch Dad with that fingertip? How much did that middle finger remember? How much did she lose? She never regained feeling there.

When we hold someone's hand, tactile nerve fibers hum alive, convening to dispense information about the size, shape, and texture of the hand we hold. These nerves trail down from our brains, tunneling through the spinal cord and spider-webbing out to the extremities, where they terminate in mechanoreceptors buried beneath the skin ("mechano" as in mechanical, produced by machines, moved by weights and measures; "receptor" as in to receive, to be given, as in gift). We read the gift of touch automatically, methodically. The robotic feelers of the hand catalogue a wealth of information, telling us if the hand we're holding is soft and smooth, like my mom's, or heavy and rough, like my brother's, or squeezing and timid, like mine. The hand's mechanoreceptors are extremely adept at calculating what a hand holding ours is like. They're considered low-threshold because even light, brief stimulation arouses them.

For a year, I dated a lot of men. I wanted to be lovable, to love. I wanted to want to hold someone's hand. I wanted someone to read my body like my parents read each other. The men were all kind and all wrong. The pilot bought me ice cream after we watched a folk band at a pub. The poet liked to walk with me at midnight. The guitar player took me to a market, then for a drive-through slushie. Or was that the teacher? They blended together, vaguely happy with their worlds. Whenever they began to open up, I'd feel the distance stretch out between us, a map unfolding to reveal more miles. One was wistful about dreams he'd let go, one recounted his parents' cold divorce, another ruminated on the separation from his wife. After a month, maybe two, I would stop responding to their messages. I'm too busy, I'd say. Or, It's not working out. Or, I'm seeing other people. Every excuse boils down to this: I wouldn't let them get close.

In LA, in Chinatown, an old man sat at a plastic foldout table, an empty chair across from him. I was twenty, visiting a friend, and that day I moved in and out of shops, thinking about buying pens or hairclips but always coming back to the old man, drawn toward him sitting alone, waiting. He smiled and waved. Red paper lanterns swayed in the breeze. Eventually, I gave him twenty dollars, and he took my cold hand, held the back of it like he was cupping an oyster shell. His other hand danced over the meat of my palm. He was gentle, tracing my lines, feeling for bumps, explaining the topography of my life. What must it have been like, to read the stories of people's lives day in and day out, to see their lifetimes unfold in creased skin? He was silent as he read my story. My lifeline dipped from the stretch of skin between my thumb and pointer to the bottom of my palm, where it centered over the linkage of hand to wrist. My head line started in the same place, but ended somewhere else, petering out at the palm's edge beneath my pinkie. And my heart line was the top line, the one that interested me most. It faded into being between my index and middle finger, curving toward the outside of my palm like a hill grading down, landing above my head line and cutting deep at the end. The palm reader's hand hovered over mine, and he looked up, meeting my eyes. Finally, he spoke. I'd have a child at thirty-three, he said, and suffer a great loss when I was young. I would have money, but no love. Or maybe he said no money, but love. Years later, I can't remember.

Fingers feeling for what used to be absence, filling in the emptiness, the soft web of flesh meeting known bones. Fingertips curling around the back of a hand, thumb over thumb. Knuckle next to knuckle next to knuckle, et cetera. Palm to palm, the soft meat of one hand meeting the soft meat of another. Does lifeline pair to lifeline? Do the creases match up? Two hands so close you can't see inside them.

Our second date was also in the evening. There was a nearby lake that was open during the day for swimming that had floating docks and lifeguard stands and floating ropes to mark off areas, things like that, but we went there after it was closed and went swimming. We broke into it and went swimming. We had a picnic dinner and went swimming. I don't know why he wanted to do it, but that's what we did.

Mom wears three rings every day: her wedding ring, her engagement ring, and Dad's wedding ring. They sit stacked on one finger. The wedding rings are simple gold bands, no embellishment, and the engagement ring has a square diamond centered. Dad's ring is loose, so Mom keeps the other two on top to hold it in place; it would slip off without them. Sometimes people ask about Dad's ring, people who don't know, friends of friends, grocery store clerks, or waitresses at dinner. "It's my husband's," Mom says. How does she explain she's married to someone she can no longer touch? She doesn't like the word "widow," the way it crawls out of the mouth, the way it tastes like burnt caramel, a sticky sweetness overcooked.

In college, poring over diagrams in my cinderblock dorm room to study for a test, I learned that the most common mechanoreceptors of glabrous (hairless, smooth) skin are Meissner's corpuscles. In my textbook, Meissner's corpuscles looked like the pads of fingers, ovaled capsules hiding a mess of cells inside. These receptors keep busy. They relay almost half of all the sensory information from the human hand to the larger nervous system, constantly stringing their messages up the telephone lines of neuronal axons. Beside them on the page, Pacinian corpuscles, a different kind of mechanoreceptor, looked like fat onions, circles of cells circling circles of cells. These receptors account for only 10 to 15 percent of the hand's mechanoreceptors, much less than Meissner's, but the two are structurally similar, and together, they do a lot of feeling. In my notes, I wrote: these types of receptors are particularly attuned to the texture of the object felt.

What is the texture of loss?

In a picture, I hold a small, soft puppy. I bend my neck to nuzzle her nose, hold her in my lap with two hands. One brushes her floppy ear, the other reaches around from chest to back. I wear Pikachu pajamas and a beaded bracelet that still has the price tag on it. I'm sitting in Dad's lap, and his head is bent over mine. With one hand, he brushes the hair out of my face and tucks it behind my ear; with the other, he reaches around my waist to help hold the puppy in place. Dad wears a white turtleneck and circular wire-rimmed glasses. My fingers are pudgy and soft, still growing into themselves, and Dad's knuckles look almost swollen in comparison. A green vein climbs from one knuckle up toward the wrist. He wears a black sports watch and a gold wedding band.

When my parents were together in a room, even if they had their backs turned to each other, even if they were engrossed in different conversations, even if they couldn't see each other, it felt as though they were connected by an invisible fishing line. Doing the dishes, cooking dinner, unloading the dishwasher, their bodies unconsciously reached for each other. Dad opened and Mom leaned into the embrace. One hand in the suds-filled sink, she looped the other around the back of his neck as he fastened his arms around her. A kiss on the lips, a squeeze of the hand. Their bodies finished each other's sentences.

On a date, a man's eyes widened. He touched my hand. "It's my college ring," I said. I wore it on my ring finger partially as a joke, that is, married to my education, but also because the idea of being engaged felt ludicrous to me. What else was I going to put on that finger? The ring is gold with my college crest emblazoned on it. "Lux Libertas" it reads, with two fake diamonds on either side. On the back, inscribed inside the ring where my date couldn't see, my name is engraved in cursive. I didn't tell him about the hidden letters, but I let him touch my hand. We were eating dinner at a midrange Mexican restaurant, one with cloth napkins and baskets full of thin chips. He reached over his silverware and pulled my hand beside the fake candle to look. His touch lingered for a moment, his fingertips finding the underside of mine, his thumb beneath my ring. My body froze. The softness of his fingers, the gentle way he held me: it was the only thing. I felt it, even when he pulled away.

Horatio Nelson, the revered British naval officer, met Emma, Lady Hamilton, in 1798, and they quickly fell in love. This love was inconvenient (they were both married) but undeniable. Three years later, Emma had a daughter with Nelson, Horatia, and moved from Italy to England to set up house with him. But in 1805, at the Battle of Trafalgar, Nelson died. His last words, spoken to lieutenant Thomas Hardy, were, "Take care of my dear Lady Hamilton, Hardy; take care of poor Lady Hamilton." His body was placed in a barrel of brandy, preserved until he could be brought back to England, where, when he was pulled from the liquid and his clothing catalogued, soldiers would note a simple gold ring, one of a pair, the other around Lady Hamilton's finger, both carved with two hands clasped.

My parents said "I love you" every day. In the morning, Dad would wake up first, get dressed, brush his teeth, and kiss Mom. "Have I told you yet today that I love you?" He'd say. Mom would smile under the blue comforter. "No," she'd say.

"Okay, I love you," he'd say. When he was happy, smiling, his whole face shifted. His cheeks rounded, and his eyes squinted. "I love you, too," Mom replied.

Your dad was the first and only person that I really loved. And I was old. But I was somebody who: I was going to get my degree, I had other things to do. It wasn't that I didn't have fun; I went out with people. But there was never anybody that I was seriously interested in, and so I didn't date people for very long. And I probably pushed people away and put up barriers: it was self-protective. I wouldn't let anybody get close. And so your dad was the first person that I would allow to get that close.

This week, I was cutting hard bread for my gumbo, the crust rough beneath my fingertips, when the knife slipped, the bread flinched, and I sliced my finger open. It was a small incision below the nail, small but deep. At first, it didn't bleed. Then, it did. I wrapped the band-aid so tightly my fingertip turned purple. The next morning, I unwrapped the bandage and checked for blood. The cut looked shriveled from the compression, a little puckered from the loss of blood. The wound looked closed, so I took the bandage off and walked to a local market. I saw two friends and made my way toward them to say hello, swiveling past ripe avocados and a bushel of fresh flowers. I don't remember what I said, but I remember, in the middle of my rambling, one of them stopped me. "Maddie," she said, "you're bleeding." The blood was everywhere—dripping down my hand, staining the cuff of my sweatshirt, pouring out. I pushed a napkin against the cut, ordered a cookie, and called my mom. "You'll never guess what I did," I said.

On my bedside table rests a picture of my mom in her doctoral gown, blue hood hanging off her shoulders. Her hands overlay each other, holding a plastic cup of lemonade, and she wears a single gold ring. Her skin is tight, with two veins embroidered on her right hand. Her wrists are covered by the dark gown, so her hands float in front of her body. The tip of her pinkie touches the tip of her pinkie. Her ring finger covers the nail of her ring finger. Her index finger covers the nail of her index finger. One thumb touches the rim of the cup. The other is out of sight. I imagine Dad took this picture of her. From the way she is smiling, full and broad, without restraint, it must have been Dad who took this picture.

In a photo, Mom recognizes me by my hands. They hover over a keyboard, my face out of frame. My fingers are stubby, nails painted, two rings on two fingers, one my college ring, the other my maternal great-grandmother's good-credit diamond ring. She got it when she opened a bank account decades ago, and my grandmother got it when her mother died, and my mom got it when my grandmother went into surgery, and I got it for my twentieth birthday. The diamond is small, a quick glint in the center of a square of silver that's set into the gold band. For a while, Mom wore it as an engagement ring. Dad was starting residency, Mom her fellowship, and they decided to try to match in the same place, coordinating their top choices. When they moved in together, Mom told Dad he had a year to decide if he wanted to make the relationship permanent. She knew he had dated Hilda for six years, and Mom didn't have that long to give. The next day, Dad said, "I dare you to spend the rest of your life with me." She didn't realize it was a proposal, so she laughed, and the following morning

Dad said, "You never answered me." She moved her grandmother's ring to her ring finger.

Mom's fede ring, the one she bought herself in high school, the one she gave to me in college, the one I broke, was a specific type, a gimmel fede ring. Two or three loops come together to complete a gimmel ring, gimmel from *gemellus*, meaning twin. These rings date as far back as the thirteenth century BCE, when Henry III of England presented a French count with a joint ring studded with a ruby and two emeralds. Around 1600, the gimmel ring began incorporating the clasped hands of the fede ring, and sometimes, on a third band, beneath the two hands, a heart, hidden. It's the separation, then, that makes the heart visible.

My parents had their own language, and I heard only caught consonants. The way they leaned together in the cold soccer stadium seats, the way they set the table, passing spoons and knives and forks to each other without looking or asking, the way they reached for each other's hands, naturally. And this was only the language I knew I couldn't understand. There were whole phrases, paragraphs, books that I missed.

Huddled just beneath the epidermis, the topsoil of the skin, Merkel's disks are unencapsulated mechanoreceptors, meaning they're open and vulnerable to touch. These pronged nerve endings tap into the underside of skin and account for one-fourth of the hand's mechanoreceptors. Lying in my lofted bed with my reading light heating my bare legs, I traced these receptors in my textbook as my phone buzzed with texts from boys that would remain unanswered. The disks are slow-adapting, so they don't recognize abrupt changes, not right away at least, but they pay attention to pressure, sending messages back to your body to let you know you're being held.

Our third date was the one where I actually thought the relationship could be serious. We wanted to go have a picnic again outdoors. And we were racing up the mountain from the university because we wanted to get there by sunset. But we were leaving late, and we had to go to try and get there and then hike up to the spot on the mountain to watch the sunset. And we were going to be late, and you can't hike up in the dark, let alone hike back. So that was the date when we took that picture—I told you that's one of the favorite pictures I have of your dad and me. Back then selfies weren't a thing; we had to set the camera on a timer and set it on a rock and take a picture. But we took a picture. And so that was our third date, and that's when I knew that it could be something more.

I don't know if my dad ever had his palm read. I don't remember the creases in his hands, how deep they were, where they ended or began. I wouldn't know how to interpret these landmarks even if I could recall them. All I know is this: he had a piece of lead stuck in the center of his palm, like a bird caught midflight. When he was in the fifth grade, someone threw a pencil to him, at him. It flew like a plane, parallel to the floor, zooming over cluttered desks. Dad put his hand up, like he had a question, like he was waving hello, and when the lead touched the center of his palm, he pivoted his hand downward, and the eraser slammed the desk, and the lead broke the skin. The tip of the pencil went so deep it became permanently embedded, or rather as permanent as a human life is. The spot was dark but deep, a faded black mark covered over by years of calloused skin.

At the hospital, the doctor told us "soon." Family and friends considered family stood around the bed in a circle. Light streamed through the windows. A doctor and priest thumbed Dad's pulse, waiting. Around the bed, we held each other, arms around shoulders, arms around waists. When the priest started reciting last rites, I broke the circle and reached for Dad's hand. It was cold and heavy. It felt odd, holding a hand that couldn't hold mine back, but I squeezed it tight. My palm pressed against his palm. I didn't want Dad to be scared. I didn't want him to die feeling alone.

Ruffini's corpuscles lie deep in the skin. These bundled balls of nerve fibers respond to skin stretching, like hands opening, closing, opening again. They account for 20 percent of the hand's mechanoreceptors, and though they aren't well understood, we know that they respond primarily not to externally but to internally generated stimuli, meaning they turn their attention inward, cataloguing the body's own movements while the outside world spins on.

After a year of rampant dating, I stopped. I never held any of their hands, not when we were walking or driving or sleeping in bed. Not in parks, at coffee shops, or during live shows. I don't regret seeing them, but I realized that love is a practice and these men were practice. I want to be open with men, not empty, so for now, that means letting them go. Slowly, they dropped off, and eventually, I was left by myself in my own life. My hands are more cold than clammy now, but the center of my palms are still always a little damp. When I'm thinking, caught in an updraft from the past, I sometimes interlace my fingers, let my hands rest in my lap or under my chin, a circuit completed.

In crowds, moving together toward their destination, a movie theater or buffet table, navigating, wherever they were, a sea of bodies, my parents held hands. They feared separation. Together, they weaved through parties, lines, entrances, and exits. They held hands in motion, but they held hands standing still, too. It was less a signal to others that they were together and more about how it made them feel. Their fingers interlocked, palms pressed together, mechanoreceptors firing, they felt connected. They felt safe. They wanted to feel the other beside them, always.

The sky is orange, the dying light of a sunset, but most of the background is black, the shadowed side of a mountain. My parents' faces are lit up by the camera's flash. Dad wears a grey hat with a dark ribbon around the base. Mom wears a white windbreaker, Dad a blue one. Their skin is tanned and unmarked by aging, smooth and bright. Dad's smile crinkles his eyes, and Mom's lips push into laugh lines. It's the kind of happy that can't be faked. Mom leans against Dad and he tilts toward her, the beginning of a lifetime of reaching.

In my brother's truck, Mom sits in the passenger seat with me a row behind her. I'm home for a few days to visit, and I'm crying, first without noise, then with deep breaths. I'm crying because I just watched my basketball team lose in double over-time: I know that sounds silly, overblown, and it is, I know it is, but they could've won, they should've won; they deserved to win. You could see how much they wanted it in their quivering muscles, their sweat-gleaned bodies. They lost at the buzzer, and so I'm crying as we drive to a late dinner in the dark be-cause desire means nothing in the face of loss. Mom doesn't turn her head. She keeps looking at the streets illuminated by staggered lamps and stoplights and I keep crying. She keeps looking ahead, but she reaches her arm backward, around her seat and toward me. In the dark, without looking, without turning, she finds my hand and squeezes. I was wrong: desire means everything in the face of loss. She squeezes my hand, and I squeeze back.

ON THE LOVE OF HILLS

old your foot, sole turned inward. Prod the soft flesh with your thumbs, kneading the thick skin, pushing aside muscle and sinew in favor of something harder. Search until you find, coupled beneath the ball of the foot, two peas. These are embedded in the fibrous tissue that connects the big toe's muscle to the big toe's bones. Two calcified peas keep the foot from breaking, keep the muscle from tearing, keep the body moving. Except these bones are not two calcified peas; they are two small bones, each a little caved in on top, the outer bone slightly larger and longer, the central bone more rounded, both bones, both misshapen, hard, different-sized bones. These bones, called sesamoids (like "sesame," like "sesame seed"), sit beneath the big toe bone and act as a fulcrum. They're protection from the rough ground, from loose gravel and slippery mud, and they act as shock absorption when running, the pounding of soft body against immovable ground mitigated by two small bones the size of corn kernels. They take forces up to three times your body weight. Think about that: if you weigh one hundred pounds, three hundred pounds of force are held up by bones smaller than an earlobe. Such small things to bear all that weight.

I've been thinking about sesamoids because mine can't take as much as they used to. I run every other morning, snaking my way along Tucson's mostly dried up Rillito River. The riverbed is brown, the paved trail swept clean each week, and yet, as I run, I find: yellow leaves dropped from ocotillo, chalked messages ("Cookie is a bitch!"), beer cans, broken glass, splattered piss, bird shit. I try to pay attention to the trail, to the small pools of dirty water still like glass, to the bend where green overtakes dirt, to the bikers tossing off, "on your left," but mostly I don't register any of it. A tenth of a mile in and I feel my sesamoid grinding against soft tissue, tears in tender flesh pushing blood vessels to open, white cells pooling around the bone, heat squeezing the ball of my foot. A tenth of a mile in and every thought I have is poked through by pain, a plastic grocery bag losing its bottom. Wrinkled and red *Thank you, Thank you, Thank you* punctured by the small bones in my left foot. The tendon around one of my sesamoids becomes inflamed as bone frictions against it. Inflammation builds as I run further, and a dull pain surges with every push. It's a pain I seek.

The rabbi dropped the bone in water, but it didn't dissolve. He threw it in blue fire, but it didn't burn. He shoved it in a mill, centered it on an anvil, and struck it with a hammer. The anvil cleaved, the hammer shattered, but the bone remained unbroken. Around 210 CE, Rabbi Uschaia spoke of the luz, a bone named after a nut, an almond. The bone, when plucked from a dead body and planted in soft earth, would regrow body and soul on the day of judgment. In the Middle Ages, non-Jewish scholars picked up the myth. Some marked the luz as the last vertebra in the spinal column, some as the butterflied bone tailing off the spine, as the curling tail pointing between the legs, and some marked the resurrection bone as one of the foot's sesamoids.

Sesamoids, technically, are bones connected to muscles by tendons. They're different than most bones, which simply touch each other at joints. The foot's sesamoids are not the only sesamoids in the body; there are sesamoids in the wrist, the hand, the neck, and ear, but like the rabbi, I'm interested in the ones that sit beneath a planted metatarsal bone: the foot's sesamoids.

In 1543, Vesalius, the father of modern human anatomy, wrote the landmark medical text *De Humani Corporis Fabrica*, translated as "On the Fabric of the Human Body." In it, he traced the sesamoid's rumored powers to magicians and occultists, filtered the story through different traditions, but in the end, it doesn't matter that the origins were blurred; he threw this mythology aside, wrote, "The dogma which asserts that man will be regenerated from this bone . . . may be left for elucidation to those philosophers who reserve to themselves alone the right to free discussion and pronouncement upon the resurrection and the immortality of the soul." He didn't want murky myths. He wanted only the hardened thing, the bone itself.

Sesamoids develop in utero, a fact discovered in 1736, and yet in 1803, in 1872, up until 1892, over a hundred and fifty years later, many physicians believed these small bones developed in response to trauma. Doctors thought the cumulative weight of a body walking and standing on solid ground would tear at the tendons and rip open muscle fibers, a rope breaking by threads. They believed that the growth of the foot's sesamoids, the growing ball of bone, would protect the body from its own violence.

It started with a pop. If I trace my pain back far enough, it didn't start with chronic overuse, the dull dailiness of living; it came from a quick rip. I played soccer growing up, and one game, when I was in eighth grade, I cut too hard, too quick, too fast. I pushed off to the right, and my body followed, head, torso, and legs swinging out, but my toe box stayed put. My foot didn't leave the soft grass fast enough, and the big toe joint hyperextended, bent too far with too much force behind it, so the ligaments around the joint, the soft tissue around the sesamoid, tore. My body ripped. I kept moving till the end of the match. We won, and I taped an ice bag to my foot.

The next day, the swelling was worse. The pink blob beneath my ankle didn't respond to rest, ice, compression, or elevation. I pushed a finger into the tender skin, looking for bone, finding the squish of inflammation. That morning, at the dining room table, with the light dropping through fingerprinted windows and my foot in his hands, Dad kneeled on the floor, head bent as he palpated for pain. He felt for guideposts in the metatarsals, pushed back against my hallux, said, "Tell me when it hurts."

"Dad, it hurts."

Dad used to run every Thursday afternoon with Mike and Dell, two old men from the neighborhood, one an artist and the other a former marine. In the beginning, they all ran the same loop, but Mike and Dell ran one way and Dad ran the other, three points meeting, then leaving. I don't know how many times they passed each other before their faces became familiar, before they recognized Dad's green hat or he recognized Dell's long hair. I don't know how long it took before waves turned to hellos, before the meetings extended and the leavings slowed. I know they ran the same loop the same way for at least a year, under dogwood trees and past the elementary school, toward the bars downtown but not past their throw-up-splattered fronts. I know at the end, Dad hated picking up the phone, telling them his white blood cell count was too low, he couldn't run, not today. I know in the hospital Mike couldn't enter the room; he sobbed in the hallway, then left. Dad was cremated, so there was no coffin, but on the funeral program Mike and Dell were listed as honorary pallbearers. I know it felt wrong, seeing them in suits.

I didn't start running until after Dad died. At first, it was hard: heavy breathing, sore muscles, and slow mile times. But I adapted. Now, I run faster, run farther, still with sore muscles. Time drains away as my foot hits the pavement, hits the pavement, hits the pavement. My body strikes my body, bone against ligament, hardness into softness. The inflammation builds; my bones suffocate, blood vessels gasp. The pain swells.

After three, four, six miles, I walk back to my car and perform the same routine. I press my foot against the parking lot curb and lean into the hypotenuse of my shoe, stretching one calf, then the next. I pull one ankle up above the other leg's knee, let the side of my shoe's Brooks swoosh imprint on my thigh. I make a figure four with my lower body, then bend like I'm sitting in a chair. I stretch my glutes, then hug my knees, stretching my hamstrings. I shake out my arms, take off my sweaty running hat, and drive home. Sometimes a park worker witnesses this monotony, but typically, there is no one there to see it.

I mostly run by myself, preferring to be alone with my pain, but when friends ask to join, I don't know how to explain this to them, how to tell them this is my time with my dad. Instead, I send them pictures of the dead birds I find on the trail. In one month, I find half a dozen. I have no idea why I find so many; they seem to have died from different injuries at different times, but there are similarities, too. These birds are always small, small enough to be cradled in one palm. Their stiffened legs crack the air, avian rigor mortis, but their feathers look the same as when they were alive, soft along the chest, scything at the tail. Sometimes their wounds are obvious, chests pierced open to purpling red. Sometimes I have to circle their bodies, searching until I find the pinpoint of hurt.

Ligaments can stretch only so far. Rewind to the moment my toe stayed behind and my body kept moving. Press play. The tissue connecting my sesamoid to my metatarsal frays, and open-fisted neurons slingshot the sensory information from my foot to the base of my spine, the indent that I inexplicably bruise every two months or so. The message slips between my vertebrae and into my spine's interior column of gray matter, coursing through my S1 sacral (as in sacred) nerve, pinning luz to luz through injury. It climbs the coil of nerves like a devoted student in gym class and rings the bell in my thalamus, which relays the sound to my somatosensory cortex, the distorted feeling map of my body fitted onto brain folds, a place where my lips are huge, my palms wide, shoulders narrow. It's a place where the body's smallness has no correlation to its sensation. Here, the message sent from my big toe is finally plugged in, and a marquee lights up: PAIN.

This action occurs in less than a second, but the history of pain predates my own. After a long run, I sat on my bed, foot throbbing, and read *Pnin*. "The history of man is the history of pain!" wrote Nabokov. In the third century BCE, in *Of Parts of Man*, Hippocrates, or someone whose text is gathered under his name, wrote that pain is created by opposites, "through cold and heat, excess and want." Some five hundred years later, Erasistratus separated sensory nerves from motor nerves and suggested that pain and the active response to it live in different lanes; he learned this by cutting open live criminals, knifing into bleeding flesh to "capture in the raw what nature had kept hidden." Centuries and lifetimes later, Galen marked the three steps of pain: (1) the reception of the exterior, (2) the connection to the interior, and (3) the perception of the sensation. As in (1) the rough road (2) hitting the foot (3) felt as throb. Galen knew that pain could be visual and auditory, but he thought the greatest pains came from touch, specifically from a swift and sharp break, a coming together or breaking apart. The foot against pavement, the foot in the air. Numbness, he said, is the opposite of pain.

At the hospital, I laid in a dark room, and a lead apron pinned my body down as a machine outlined the bones in my foot. The X-ray technician told me to stay still as the machine buzzed, then clicked, buzzed, then clicked. I felt cold. Dad stood in a separate room with the orthopedic surgeon, both of them behind a lead-lined wall as what lay hidden behind muscle and skin rose in silver on thick film. At the time, I didn't consider it, but it must've scared Dad, not being able to fix my foot.

I rarely went to the doctor growing up. I was a doctor's kid, so Dad treated almost everything: ankle sprains, Osgood-Schlatter, a head broken open. He bought me a brace, showed me how to lace it up tight. Before bed, he taught me how to stretch the muscles pulling on my kneecaps (the largest sesamoid bone in the body); he helped me release the pain built into growth. In the living room, he held my opened skin together while the liquid stitches dried. The screaming mouth carved into my skull stayed shut.

At the doctor's, the X-ray didn't show any breaks. This surprised the surgeon, who'd marveled at my swollen foot. "You can walk on it?" he asked. I nodded. My foot had gotten so large I could no longer wear normal shoes: no sneakers, flats, or flip-flops for me. Swelling deformed my body, and I could only shove the inflamed mass into rubber Crocs, shoes built to be too big and too loose. At school, after eating lunch, I'd sit in the physical trainer's office with my foot in a bucket filled with ice water. I'd come back after school to do it again, feel the sting of cold give way to numbness. During practice, I moved the bucket outside to sit with the team, changing the water once all the ice melted. Half a week later, my foot wasn't better, but I was back on the field. The trainer taped my toe as best she could in an attempt to immobilize the sprain. I shouldn't have played, but I was a varsity starter and it was playoffs. We lost, and I iced my foot all the way home.

⁣⁣⁣⁣*＠∂∂∂∂⁣*

Ligaments are mostly wet: two-thirds water, one-third solids. Collagen accounts for most of the dry weight, with other proteins rounding out the arid mass. At their most basic, ligaments are used for stabilization, but as more force is applied to one, its fibers are stretched taut, tensed and at their thinnest. When I pushed off, the ligament studded with two sesamoids was pulled and pulled. Neighboring fibers were recruited to help carry my weight, and then, those fibers were stretched taut. My body stretched between two points, where I was and where I was going. When the force of moving became too much, the ligament tore.

My body responded to this tear as most bodies do to soft tissue injury—with inflammation, proliferation, and tissue remodeling. First, blood cells congregated, leaching growth factors, crowding the injury, burgeoning against skin. My foot felt hot; it ballooned. Then, fibroblasts (cells that synthesize scaffolds) bloomed, building scar tissue with more blood vessels and fat than healthy tissue. They laid down the railroad tracks toward recovery. Finally, the body braided spindly collagen fibers into place. These fibers almost looked normal. On the surface, they seemed healthy. But histologically, biochemically, and biomechanically, the replacement tissue was more scar than not.

The period after this rebuilding is crucial. The tissue can adapt and strengthen, relearning how to hold the weight of a body, or it can fail, snap. Incrementally increasing force, testing the surface tension of repair, can strengthen the ligament, but returning to activities before the injury has healed increases the risk of reinjury. You have to wait for the symptoms to disappear, for the pain to leave before resuming life. Still, there is only so much caution can do. Too much move-

ment, not enough—I wonder if it truly matters. Once a ligament tears, it is more likely to tear again.

When I feel the thin soles of Converse sneakers, taste the cool-
ness of mint chip ice cream, smell the sea-salt air, I hurt. I'm
always hurting. He wore them to his wedding; it was his favorite flavor; we scattered his ashes in the ocean. The shadow-
thought to everything is this: my dad is dead. It's why the
scuffed voice of David Byrne pinches me behind the nose, why
the bite of Blue Moon beer kicks at the backs of my knees, why
the smell of blueberry muffins crumples me. I keep hurting,
not because I'm masochistic, but because not hurting feels
worse. Because forgetting hurts more than loss. I'm trying to
explain that every pain is a resurrection.

But the pain in my body isn't a neat metaphor—it's real. I
take a step, and my sesamoid pokes into soft tissue, the small
dagger of self stabbing self. Imagine walking everywhere with
a nail pushed through the bottom of your shoe, sharp metal
digging into pink muscle and knifing against bone, blood loose
like quarters dropped into a purse. How can anyone understand anyone else's pain? My pain is not an image, an allegory,
a literary symbol. My pain is neurons screaming. It is shouting
in every step. It is constant, everyday pain living in my body.
Feel it.

I have two runner friends, Ro and Margo. Neither of them
knew my dad, but Ro flies across the country one weekend to
run three miles with me. Margo lives in the same city as me,
and every month she gives me a new running nutrient (first,
electrolyte pills, then orange gel and pre-run smoothie ad-
ditives). Ro is on T and worries their vagina will just fall out
one day. On the phone, I ask them to keep any ovary innards

in a jar and call it "girlhood." They only find this marginally funny. Margo starts a new medication to regulate her period. She worries she can't get pregnant and ushers me into a public bathroom to look at her clotted period blood. "Does this look normal to you?" she asks. The bathroom isn't well lit, but the flimsy metal doors reverberate the overhead fluorescent light. We lean into the stall together, and she shows me her body's elegy. The blood is sticky, almost black against the white toilet paper. "That's normal for me," I say.

I can run with both of them because they see the human body as material, but I'm coming to realize they see it as ethereal too. When my grandmother has to be put into a memory care facility overnight, I start crying and Margo asks if she can hug me. I let myself be held. I feel my ribs ripple against her body, bone against muscle, hardness yielding to softness. I'd forgotten touch meant something. When Ro visits, they wear smelly toe-shoes and match their pace to mine. We stop to take pictures of a bright green praying mantis crossing the trail while we catch our breath. On my birthday, they give me a copy of the *Kaufman Field Guide to Birds of North America*, and I start identifying the dead birds.

I need to say this: it isn't about the birds; it's about spending time with these dead bodies, giving them my attention, my care. I'd always seen love in procedures, routines, and checklists checked off each day. When Margo sent me a twelve-week training plan, she was saying, *I love you*. When Ro told me to focus on a spot in the distance, run to there, then choose another, another, another, they were saying *I will always love you*. I didn't tell my friends how I matched cellphone pictures to meticulous illustrations, but in truth, I wouldn't have done it if not for them. Their fuel suggestions and stretching demonstrations gave me permission to catalogue the body, my body. They showed me it was possible to love each piecemeal part of the self, even the bits prone to breaking, so I started looking at others to learn how to better see myself.

The Kaufman guide advises looking at the shape of the bird

first; the blacked-out silhouette alone can tell you whether it's a Cassin's kingbird or Virginia's warbler. I click open a picture on my phone, note the curves of the body. I decide this bird, with its chest pecked in, is a sparrow. Next, check the underparts pattern. The field guide asks, "Is the bird streaked across the chest or down the sides, does it have a dark chest spot, or is it plain below?" The belly is white, circled by yellow, like the faded rings around my childhood bathtub. I check the head pattern and the habitat: brown stripes painted on the soft core of a hard-boiled egg, and mostly dry desert. Finally, social life. According to the book, "Sparrows (like most birds) are in pairs or family groups during nesting season, but at other seasons, some species are in flocks while others are usually solitary." The dead bird, the first one I saw, is a Savannah sparrow. It moves in loose family groups. I wonder where its kin are now.

In 1901, the first case of a divided sesamoid in humans was recorded. Most of us have two sesamoids in each foot, each one nestled underneath the ball of our foot like training wheels on a bicycle, but sometimes one wheel separates into two, an uneven tricycle. In 1901, a chunk of clay fell on a forty-year-old's foot, and the surgeon, Schunke, noted the presence of three bones where usually there were two. He called this division a fracture and "cured" it by immobilizing the patient's foot. In 1904, a different forty-year-old patient fell three feet and landed hard on one foot. A different surgeon, Marx, removed one of the three sesamoids in surgery; the procedure was declared a success, but in 1907, 1908, these partitioned bones were marked as a developmental division, a natural progression from one to two. Now, most surgeons recognize this third sesamoid, this division of one into two to make three, as a frequent occurrence. Still, among similar studies, the incidence of divided sesamoids varies wildly from 16 percent to 4 percent to one in one thousand. There is still so much unknown. I wish I could find the X-ray of my foot to see how many bones sit beneath my metatarsal, but no matter how many boxes I rifle through, the image eludes me.

Bipartite sesamoids ("bi" meaning two, "partire," to part) develop in children seven to ten years old. I already would've learned to ride a bike but still would be waiting for my period. The larger, more central sesamoid is often the one to part, though "part" isn't necessarily the right word. It's addition, not division. A second ossification center builds beside the already present bone, cartilage cells growing bigger and lining themselves up. As the newly congregated cells become further separated, calcareous material flows between them like water slipping between stones. The cells form columns, then rows. The inner cartilage cells are cut off from nutrition by the hardening, calcified matrix. These cells die, leaving open space in the center, a hollowed bone. This new bone now sits beside its twin, a channel flowing between them. Two sesamoids are now three. This is not to say that fractures can't occur to sesamoids; they can, and they do. But they occur less frequently than bipartite sesamoids, meaning twoness is not always a symptom of trauma. Sometimes these bones simply grow to help support the body's weight, meaning growth can mirror brokenness.

I remember running with Dad only once. I was in high school and angry about something; I needed to move. I sat on the couch, lacing up my tennis shoes, when I asked Dad if he wanted to run with me. He took the stairs two at a time and came back with his shoes in hand. I think we ran a different route than the one he ran with Mike and Dell, but I'm not sure; I don't know the specifics because though he asked me to run with them many times, I never said yes. (Why not? I was a teenager; I had homework and friends.)

Dad and I ran over cracked concrete, tree roots pushing up thick slabs. We ran toward the bars downtown but turned around before we reached them. Dad wore his short running shorts, which normally embarrassed me, but I was too focused on my lifting anger to be concerned. I set the pace, but I didn't know my body well enough; I thought intensity could last forever. Dad was fine, sometimes poking open conversation, asking about my friends, my day, school, but my breath was ragged and I could only manage half sentences. I was sweat slicked and red faced before we even reached the hill.

It's the hill I remember best, the one I love the most, though that wasn't true at the time. When we reached the base of the climb, a neighborhood street draped with oaks and lined with trash cans, Dad started yelling, "I love hills!" He kept yelling as we climbed. I smiled despite myself. I knew from Mom's marathon stories that he would do this, but it thrilled me to hear him say it. I was annoyed and tired, gasping for breath, but I was happy too.

The evolutionary hypothesis of pain suggests that the association of pleasure with helpful situations and pain with harmful ones is the result of natural selection. Put simply, pain helps us survive. Walking on hot pavement hurts because it damages tissue, burns cells alive, scorches open membrane walls, and deteriorates sticky proteins; we feel the pain of it because our body wants to protect itself, wants us to stop, move, put on shoes.

To clarify, pain is not just sensation but the motivation to stop it, too. At least twenty people have been born with a mutated SCN9A gene, one that misfolds the $Na_V1.7$ protein critical for the function of pain-reporting neurons. People who can't feel pain don't respond to it, and their life expectancy is subsequently cut short, a ribbon snipped. Often eternally painless people die from tissue damage, from unknowingly harming the self. They can stand on the pavement while their feet sizzle, the smell of flesh like rich charcoal with a copper top note. They can stand there until they melt to bone, and still, they will feel nothing. They lack pain, a defense mechanism meant to alert us to the body's injuries.

Of course, sometimes, rather than feeling no pain, we feel too much. This is safer in the long run. Vomiting after a meal free of toxins is unpleasant, but failing to vomit when a toxin is present means death. This past year, I spent thirty-six hours over the rim of a toilet. I vomited my lunch, then my breakfast, then water and water. I vomited bile. I vomited nothing. I took antinausea medication that made me drowsy. I climbed into bed, draped a towel like a bib around my shoulders, and still, every hour, I rushed to the toilet, dazed, heaving until I thought my ribs would snap like an oyster pried open. I probably ate some harmful bacteria, but even if I didn't, even if my body overreacted and I heaved for nothing, even if my mouth tasted like bile for hours and my lips stayed parched for days and my chest was sore for a week, even if all this pain was for nothing, it was better than death. The body is a delicate system, often tripped by ghost intruders. We're built to suffer because it's safer.

In 2011, Dad had a kidney stone. He'd had them before: his first one came years before I was born. He drank a lot of Diet Coke, sometimes six cans a day, and he didn't drink enough water. In Dad's kidneys, salts and minerals reached for each other, becoming a stable, solid structure as more molecules held each other. For a week, he felt the crystalized ball of minerals scrape down his ureter, catching the sides of the tube, roughing the transitional epithelium. Talking with another doctor at work, eating meatloaf at dinner, working through a math problem with me, he'd fold while clutching his side, a house of cards falling. Then, he would straighten, pick up the dropped rope of his sentence. The pain came in waves, but it stayed for days. The doubling over became so intrinsic to his

life that after he finally passed the stone, the hard rock slipping into the toilet and clinking against porcelain, he asked for
songs from friends, family, and coworkers. I helped him burn
CDs for everyone, and he called the compilation "Nephrolithi-
asis." The track list included "Papa was a Rollin' Stone," "Like
a Rolling Stone," and "Stuck in the Middle with You." Pain became a pleasant memory. He switched from Diet Coke to diet
lemonade. He went to work at 5 a.m., ran at 4 p.m., came to my
soccer games at six. Life went on for months, uninterrupted.
Then, the pain came back.

For a month, he doubled over, clutching his side, clench-
ing his teeth. Sentences were cut short, left that way. He sat
on the couch with a heating pad as he wrote patient notes. He
laid down more. One night, he woke crying. Mom looked at
him, his body contorted under sheets, face collapsing in on itself, and read the story his body was telling him. She knew his
pain was not livable. They drove to the emergency room. The
roads were dark and mostly empty. The next morning, they
were home, tired. The stone wasn't moving; they needed more
tests. They went back to the hospital. They bought flights to
Johns Hopkins. More tests, they said.

Every night that week, while they holed up in a Baltimore
hotel room and my brother and I went to school, we video
chatted to recount our days. My cousin had moved down from
Ohio to live with us and go to nursing school, so the three of
us ate dinner after we talked with Mom and Dad. I don't remember what we made, maybe macaroni and cheese, spa-
ghetti, broccoli-stuffed chicken. One day at school, over lunch,
a friend asked how my dad was. It hadn't occurred to me to
worry. "He's fine," I said, "They come back this weekend." I still
didn't worry. At the airport, Mom and Dad rolled their luggage
to the curb. Dad hugged me a little too long, a little too tightly.
Our sternums pressed against each other, bone connecting to
bone before I pulled away. The rest is too painful to write.

The brain modulates pain. The prefrontal cortex, anterior cingulate cortex, insula, and amygdala, the hypothalamus, periaqueductal grey, rostral ventromedial medulla, and dorsolateral pons send fingers of nerves down the brainstem to the spinal cord, plucking at the pain or quieting the note. After receiving the PAIN signal, the brain can underline it, add exclamation marks, or it can erase the word itself.

This, too, was conserved through evolution, an unconscious selection supporting survival. When you're running from a bear, it doesn't help to feel the pain of a leg torn open, the topography of a thigh exposed. So when, thousands of years later, I'm running on the field, I don't feel the pain of a ligament sawed through; I keep running. Of course the flip side of this is true too. When I limp into the locker room, I stop listening to my coach and start thinking about the throbbing in my foot, and the pain increases. I start to grimace. When we have time to assess the wound, the body draws our attention inward. We hurt.

Whatever has our attention has priority processing in the brain. When we turn toward pain, the brain calculates how much attention we should give it, how salient the stimuli is. The body asks questions: How attractive is this? Should I approach or back away? What does it feel like to inch closer? Attention increases the experience of pain; distraction begins to numb it.

There is a conscious, cognitive element too. We can decide whether an external signal is harmful or helpful. Experienced runners find pleasure in muscle fibers breaking and rebuilding while beginners worry irreparable damage has occurred. I feel the soft unraveling in my legs, the threads fraying and shredding, and I love it. We decide what pain means to us.

Halfway through my run this morning, I notice how much I am sweating. I've just squeezed an orange gel packet from

Margo into my mouth, let the sweet glob of citrus slip down my throat like an oyster, and as I throw the empty pouch away, I inhale. I smell myself, acrid and sweet; I know that to most other people, I would smell repulsive, but I love it, the way my body spreads itself into the air, mixing with the dry dust particles. I can feel the places where it used to wet my body, the salty wash it leaves on my arms, over my collarbone. I always wear the same hat when I'm running, a green one with Dad's college crest trimmed into it. Over the weeks, the crown of the hat stiffens and pales as my sweat dries into the fabric. I wait too long to wash it. This sweat is one of the reasons I don't wear Dad's running hat, though it hangs in my closet next to mine. Sometimes I smell the lining of his cap, hoping some particle of his sweat will still be there. I press my nose into the fabric, convince myself the musk is there. It's there.

As I round the dried river's curve, I look into the basin. The edges are rough, jagged like ripped skin. Some trees root into the steep sides, but most carve into the open space below. I look at the still puddles pitted into the bed. I've been running this route for over three months, and it never occurred to me that the suggestion of dried water was an essential companion. I always run by water; even the absence of water contains the memory of wetness. I think of Dad's ashes, scattered in the ocean on a hot afternoon. Whenever I'm near water, even if it's not an ocean, even if there's no salt to speak of, even if there is no logic to suggest Dad's particles tangle in it, I think of him.

The cupped ball of my foot begins to heat up, expanding in my cushioned shoes. The pain snaps like a rubber band; I feel the pullback, the release. The sting is sweet, like hot honey poured over lips, slipped down the throat. I feel the contours of my body, inner and outer, the tips of my ears, the drop in my esophagus, my ribs, knees, ankle, my sesamoid grinding into ligament, a dull knife sawing thick meat. Beside me, the river is wet, the result of an unseasonable rain. My body jostles through the world, bones bouncing against muscle, ligaments bumping, shaking themselves loose as they meet asphalt, thin air, slow wind. Under the shadow of a bridge, with cars clacking overhead, I see white feathers and cleaned, hollow bones. The bones gleam white, even in the darkness. The feathers look soft against the concrete. Surrounded by absence, the remainder palpates for presence. I smile as my pain aches open, *Hi, Dad.*

ACKNOWLEDGMENTS

This book was supported by a Monson Arts' residency, where it evolved toward its final form. "Still Hearts" won the Literary Award in Creative Nonfiction and originally appeared in *Ninth Letter.* "On the Love of Hills" appeared in *Fourth Genre,* and an earlier version of "Hyperbaric, or How to Keep a Wound Alive" appeared on *It's Lit with PhDJ.* All illustrations are courtesy of Kristina Alton.

Much of this manuscript was completed at the University of Arizona in the MFA program, and it would not exist without the time and support afforded to me by the program. Special thanks to Ander Monson for your unwavering support and encouragement; this book would be one tenth as weird without your guidance. Thanks to Kate Bernheimer, Susan Briante, and Alison Hawthorne Deming. Thanks to Thomas Mira Y Lopez for your early thoughts in shaping this book. Thanks also to my cohort and friends, especially Lee Anne Gallaway-Mitchell, Katie Gougelet, Raquel Gutiérrez, Miranda Trimmier, Lucy Kirkman, Hea-Ream Lee, and Katerina Ivanov Prado. Thanks to Eshani Surya and Samantha Coaxall for the ever-present text message support. Thanks to Margo Steines for sharing weird pains with me.

Thank you to Nicole Walker and Beth Snead for believing in this book. I'm so grateful to be a part of the University of Georgia Press family.

Thanks to the Thomas Wolfe scholarship at UNC–Chapel Hill, where I first felt like a writer. Special thanks to Marianne Gingher, Daisy Hernández, and Bland Simpson. Many thanks to the lifelong friends and writers I met while there, including Ro Chand, Molly McConnell, and Heather Wilson. My gratitude for Stephanie Elizondo Griest knows no bounds.

Without the support and love of my family, this book, and I, would not exist. Special thanks to the first person to welcome me into the club, Caitlin Harriford. Endless thanks to the Boggs-Price family. Thank you to Kalli Bauch and Kristin and Sam Cartin. Thank you to Maggie and Roscoe. Thank you to Aunt Cathy. Mom and Will: I will never be able to express how grateful I am for your love. It is everything to me. Dad, thank you for everything you've given me and continue to give. I love you.

Ned Stuckey-French, *One by One, the Stars: Essays*

John Griswold, *The Age of Clear Profit:
Collected Essays on Home and the Narrow Road*

Joseph Geha, *Kitchen Arabic: How My Family Came
to America and the Recipes We Brought with Us*

Lawrence Lenhart, *Backvalley Ferrets:
A Rewilding of the Colorado Plateau*

Sarah Beth Childers, *Prodigals: A Sister's Memoir of Appalachia*

Jodi Varon, *Your Eyes Will Be My Window: Essays*

Sandra Gail Lambert, *My Withered Legs and Other Essays*

Brooke Champagne, *Nola Face: A Latina's Life in the Big Easy*

Maddie Norris, *The Wet Wound: An Elegy in Essays*

Printed in the USA
CPSIA information can be obtained
at www.ICGtesting.com
JSHW021102171223
53850JS00005B/139